Ice Skating at the North Pole

*Ice Skating
at the North Pole

stories by

SENA JETER NASLUND

&

Ampersand Press / Bristol, Rhode Island

Acknowledgment is made to the following publications in which these stories first appeared:

Alaska Quarterly Review: "Ice Skating at the North Pole"
The Cimmaron Review: "The Woman Who Knocked Down Walls"
The Georgia Review: "The Perfecting of the *Valse No. 14*"
Indiana Review: "Five Lessons from a Master Class"
The Iowa Review: "Essence for Ms. Venus"
Michigan Quarterly Review: "Madame Charpentier and Her Children"

"On First Hearing Artful Singing" first appeared in the anthology *These and Other Lands* (Heartlands Fiction Collective: The Westphalia Press)

The author wishes to thank the National Endowment for the Arts, The Kentucky Arts Council and the Kentucky Foundation for Women for their support.

Cover illustration by Bob Lockhart

Library of Congress Catalog Card Number: 88-83723
ISBN 0-935331-08-5
Copyright ©1989 by Sena Jeter Naslund

first printing, October 1989

Published by Ampersand Press, Creative Writing Program, Roger Williams College, Bristol, RI 02809

This book is for Flora Lee Sims Jeter
Flora Kathryn Naslund
and for
Alan Joseph Naslund

Contents

The Perfecting of the Chopin *Valse No. 14 in E Minor*

One day last summer when I was taking a shower, I heard my mother playing the *Chopin Valse No. 14 in E Minor* better than she ever had played it before. Thirty years ago in Birmingham, I had listened to her while I sat on dusty terra cotta tiles on the front porch. I was trying to pluck a thorn from my heel as I listened, and I remember looking up from my dirty foot to see the needle of a hummingbird entering one midget blossom after another, the blossoms hanging like froth on our butterfly bush. Probably she had first practiced the *Valse* thirty years or so before that, in Missouri, in a living room close enough to a dirt road to hear wagons passing, close enough for dust to sift over the piano keys. How was it that after knowing the piece for sixty years, my mother suddenly was playing it better than she ever had in her life?

I turned off the shower to make sure. It was true.

There was a bounce and yet a delicacy in the repeated notes at the beginning of the phrase that she had never achieved before. And then the flight of the right hand up the keyboard was like the gesture of a dancer lifting her arm, unified and lilting. I waited for the double *forte*, which she never played loudly enough, and heard it roar out of the piano and up the furnace pipe to the bathroom. Perhaps that was it: the furnace pipe was acting like a natural amplifier, like a speaking tube. Dripping wet, I stepped over the tub and walked through the bathroom door to the landing at the top of the stairs. She was at the section with the alberti-like bass. Usually her left hand hung back, couldn't keep the established tempo here (and it had been getting worse in the last seven or so years), but the left hand cut loose with the most perfectly rolled over *arpeggio* I had ever heard. Rubinstein didn't do it any better.

I hurried down the steps; she was doing the repeated notes again as one of the recapitulations of the opening phrase came up. I tried to see if she had finally decided to use Joseffy's suggested fingering—2, 4, 3, 1—instead of her own 4, 3, 2, 1 on which she had always insisted. But I was just too late to see. She finished with a flourish.

"Bravo!" I shouted and clapped. The water flew out of my hands like a wet dog shaking his fur. She leaned over the piano protectively.

"You're getting the keys wet," she said, smiling.

"You played that so well!"

"Suppose the mailman comes while you're naked?"

"Didn't you think you played it well?"

"I'm improving. You always do, from time to time."

"This was SUPER."

"Thank you," she said and got up to make her second

cup of coffee.

"Did you remember to take Hydropres?" I yelled. She is quite deaf, but refuses to wear her hearing aid while she practices. *You know how music sounds over the telephone,* she said to me once; that was what a hearing aid did to sounds.

"Did you take H?" I shouted a little louder.

She threw one of her white sweaters over the Walter Jackson Bate biography of Keats. "Don't read the last two chapters late at night," she said. "It makes you too sad."

I had taken to reading about romantic poets and their poetry, too, to relieve the glassy precision of my work at the pharmaceutical lab. I left the books around, and as she had done since I was a child, she read what I read— usually two hundred pages ahead of me. I put on her sweater, its wool sticking to my damp skin.

"I took H early this morning," she continued. "Did you take A?"

Aldomet is my high blood pressure drug. She takes it, too, but not till afternoon. I take it three times a day.

"No," I said. "I've forgotten again."

And I forgot about the *Valse in E Minor.* Maybe that performance was a fluke. Maybe I was mistaken.

It was not long after this that a rock in the garden began to move. It was thigh high and pockmarked, and the pocks were rimmed with mica. The arcs of mica had the same curve as a fingernail clipping or the curve of a glittering eyelash.

Our garden was on a small scale by Louisville standards—about fifty by forty feet. We had landscaped it,

11

though—rather expensively for us. A stucco wall hung between four brick columns across the back. Herringbone brick walks were flanked by clumps of iris, day lilies and chrysanthemums so that we had spots of spring, summer and fall bloom. There was a small statue of a girl looking up at the sky and spreading her stone apron to catch the rain. The apron was a birdbath. It was that sort of yard. Pretty, costly per square foot, designed to console us for our lack of scope. I had some dwarf fruit trees across the back, in front of the stucco wall.

The previous owner had had the mica boulder placed over a large chipmunk hole so no one would accidentally step in. The placement was imperfect aesthetically, and my mother said it ought to be moved, but I didn't want to go to the bother to hire somebody to do it. Sometimes I'd see her lean against the rock, her basket full of the spent heads of iris or day lilies, or windfall apples, or other garden debris. We were neat.

One bright night when the mica was arcing in the moonlight, I saw her going out there in her pajamas. She carried one of the rose satin sofa cushions, and its sides gleamed in the light. She put the cushion on top of the rock, climbed up, and sat on it. She looked like a bird sitting on a giant egg, a maharini riding an elephant, a child on a Galapagos tortoise.

I felt unreal, frightened, standing beside the bedroom curtain peering out. And stunned. I sat down on the bed, touched another satin cushion, smoothed it, soothed it. I held the cool satin against my cheeks. My tears made dark blotches on the fabric. I wanted to lie down, to deny her madness in the garden. And I did. I turned the cushion to the dry side, lay down on it and went to sleep.

In the morning the teakettle shrieked, she poured the water for her instant coffee, called "Good Morning" to me, and all was ordinary.

When I walked in the garden, I noticed the rock had shifted. Around the base was a crescent of damp stone where crumbs of still-moist earth clung. The boulder had rotated a little, as though Antarctica on a giant globe had slipped northward a hundred miles into the South Pacific. Perhaps the rock had been more precariously balanced than I had thought. Perhaps her weight had caused it to shift—a slow-motion version of a child sitting on a big beach ball.

But from that morning I began to see a change in her health. She was tired. She was less ready to smile, and her eyes took on a hurt quality. Each day she seemed to get up later. She asked to eat out, and she ate ravenously, at Italian restaurants. She ate like a runner—huge quantities of pasta.

But the food did no good. Each day she was weaker.

And each day the ugly earthy area on the rock rose higher and higher out of the ground. What had been a slight crescent of dirt became a huge black island covering several thousand miles in the Hawaii area.

She changed her diet from high carbohydrate to high protein. I wanted to speak to her about her eating, but it was as though there was a bandage across my mouth.

I tried once, in the kitchen, to say "Mama, why are you eating in this crazy way?" But all I could say was "Mmmm, Mmmm. . . ."

She glanced at me in that quick, hurt way, and I hushed.

Then the gag seemed to change its location. Instead of being across my mouth, it seemed to be tied on top of

13

my head and to pass under my chin. It was the kind of bandage you see on the dead in nineteenth-century etchings—something to hold the jaw closed, something Jacob Marley might have been wearing when he first appeared to Scrooge. Again, I felt it in the kitchen. I tried to say "Mama, Mama, what are you doing to yourself? Why are you so tired?" But I couldn't even drop my jaw, couldn't get my mouth open for a murmur.

That night I stayed awake to watch the rock. At midnight, I knelt on my bed and peered out the window. There was no human form perched on the rock. Nevertheless I watched and watched. About 1:00, when I was quite drowsy, the rock suddenly glittered. It was as though the mica were catching light at a new angle. Sometimes this happens if a lamp is turned on in the house, or one is turned off. But there was no change in the lighting and yet this sudden sparkling, flashing out of light. My mouth tried to open in a silent and spontaneous *Oh!*, but it was as though the binding cloth were in place. I was not permitted this small gesture of surprise.

Then I saw her rise up from behind the rock. She moved very slowly. Her movement was the kind I make in dreams when I feel panic, panic and also a heaviness, an inertia that scarcely permits forward motion. Her shoulders stooping, her hands and arms hanging like weights, she slowly began to walk down the bricks toward the house. I wanted to leap to meet her, to tell her, to tell her *Nevermind. Nevermind you don't have to do it, I'll hire a crane, I'll hire the neighborhood boys, I'll hire a doctor day and night, Don't try this, here, here let me help*. But I was immobilized.

The cloths that had bound shut my jaw now bound my entire body. I could not flex my knees. I tried to heave myself off the bed; I would roll to her help. But my body was as rigid as a statue.

I was forced to remain kneeling on the coverlet, looking out the window, watching her toiling past the ruddy day lilies. At a certain point, she passed beyond my sight line. There were three small steps there; and my ears strained to tell me that she had negotiated them all right, that now she was opening the storm door, now she was coming in from the night, that she had not fallen at the last moment, that she was not lying hurt right at her own safe door, that she had not struck her head on the steps—but my hearing failed, too. All of my senses were suddenly gone, as though I had received a blow to the head.

I awoke in the early hours to a loud thunderclap. The weather was changing early. It was late summer, and the fall rains were coming. Our air seemed like the ice water you stand strips of carrots and celery in to crisp. Day lilies were drooping and the chrysanthemums straining upright, ready to grow and take over the garden. I checked the statue of the girl. Serrated yellow leaves from a neighboring elm had blown into her apron.

The boulder had rotated 180 degrees from its original position. The black cap rode at the north pole. Below it the rock was clean and traces of mica sparkled in the sunlight. But I fancied the darkness was spreading, an earthen glaciation coming down to nullify the brightness of human accomplishment.

I knew it was hopeless to attempt to ask her any questions. Even as I tried mentally to formulate an inquiry, my body stiffened. I resisted that stillness. I would not be frozen into stone in my own garden in late summer. I would not take on that terrible rigidity. I would not allow my

15

body to imagine death.

Her health began to improve, but it gave me no joy. I knew that this improvement was temporary. That August, gesturing toward the garden, a friend who raised berries told me that death was part of life; she pointed at the seasonal changes. We stood on the patio talking while the Chopin *Valse No. 14* rolled out the windows.

I explained that each time my mother played it now, it was better. Sometimes it was improved only by the way a single note was played, but suddenly that note, once dead, leaped into life. And then the next time, the notes around it would be more vital, would be like flowers straining toward the light, inspired by one of their number who had risen above them. The whole surface of the music was becoming luminous.

I told my friend that the gulf between the seasonal lives of flowers and the lives of human beings was unbridgeable. The *forte* drowned out my voice, a *forte* big enough now to fill the garden.

Our garden was the perfect place for a garden party, but I had never had one there. I preferred to have one friend over at a time, or two. But two weeks after the weather change, I discovered that invitations had been issued to almost every person of my acquaintance to join me and the chrysanthemums for a gourmet dinner. *Gourmet!* To join me *and the chrysanthemums!* They weren't ready!

As usual, I had worked late at the laboratory. When I came out to the car, the pink glow of the sunset was reflected in the windshield. Amidst the wash of pink, a folded card had been placed under the wiper: an invitation for six o'clock. It was already half-past six. There wasn't a potato chip in the house, and we'd eaten our last TV entree; I was supposed to get more on the way home. While I stood there fingering the stiff paper, I realized how many people had smiled at me that day, had said *See you later* or *Looking forward to it* or *Thanks for asking*—all mysterious, muttered fragments scattered over the day, everybody being especially gracious to me, or worse, *encouraging*.

Could I run home, maybe cook flowers? I was a very poor cook; my mother was no cook. We had long benefited from eating out and from TV dinners. They were the expensive TV dinners—pretty and tasty, even if always too salty.

As I sped home, I thought that at least my mother would be there to greet them. Like an illuminated billboard, the invitation flashed at me again. I recognized the handwriting. It was her writing. Large letters, angular, the capital A half-printed, looking like a star.

There were so many cars that I had to drive past the house looking for parking. Other latecomers—there was my supervisor—were sauntering down the sidewalks toward home. I parked almost two blocks away.

As I walked home as fast as I could, half a block away, I smelled the party. I gasped. Yes, my jaw *was* allowed to drop in amazement: *Oh!* heavenly aromas.

There was roast beef! No, not just roast beef—something richer, more savory. Beef Wellington. I could envision the pastry head of a steer decorating its flank. But the odor of bacon, too, why bacon? It couldn't be, but there was a choice of entrees, just like when we had two separate frozen Stouffers. Trout was broiling under strips of bacon. There! There was a waft of garlic butter, for escargot.

And desserts had been freshly baked. That was angel

food cake in the air, and there was the sweet cinnamon of apple brown Betty, and there, the orange liqueur that goes *flambé* with crepes suzette. She had prepared three desserts. But you can't just have main courses and desserts! Where were the vegetables? She had forgotten the vegetables. Memory *was* becoming uncertain: I *had* heard her hesitate to enter the second theme of the *Valse*.

My supervisor was poised at the head of our walk, sniffing. I shouldered past him.

"Vegetables?" I exclaimed.

"Who cares?" He inhaled deeply.

I managed to make myself enter the house quietly. There was that civilized murmur in the room. The sound you hear in the finest restaurants, the bliss of conversation elevated by the artistry of food, of the tongue bending this way and that in ecstasy.

There she stood chatting, her hearing aid in place. She who had been reclusive, a devotee of music alone, for years. I noticed there was a dusting of flour on her hands and arms, up to her elbows. She seemed unaware of the flour, stood relaxed and comfortable as though she were wearing a pair of evening gloves.

"Mother," I said, "are you all right?"

She reached out and squeezed my elbow. Her grip was steadying. "Of course," she said. "I was just telling your friend we should have parties more often. I'm enjoying myself so much."

"All this food?" I said lamely.

"I can read a book, as you know. I got down James Beard, Irma Rombauer. I hadn't looked in Fanny for years."

"Are there any vegetables?"

"Sautéed celery, new peas in sherry sauce." She

18

pointed at some covered dishes. "Here comes the mailman."

Other people began to arrive. People I had lost track of years before. How did she find them? I started to ask, but the hinge of my jaw began to resist; the familiar paralysis gently threatened. Questions had become out of order.

My salivary glands prompted me. Eat, *eat*. She had my plate ready for me—flamboyant and multi-colored. It held something of everything. When I inhaled, I seemed to levitate six or seven inches—or float, that feeling you get walking neck deep in a swimming pool on your big toes. Glancing down, I saw my food had been arranged on a new plate, the tobacco-leaf pattern that I had admired in the Metropolitan Museum catalogue. Seventy-nine dollars *per*. And each guest had one. I was rich.

One guest held no tobacco-leaf plate. Indeed, he wasn't eating. I didn't know him, had never known him, I was quite sure. He was standing beside the piano talking with mother. He was grossly fat, with reddish hair, what was left of it; he was mostly bald. Only his nose seemed familiar. It was a large and romantic proboscis, lean and humped—no, arched. They were discussing fingering. Mother was drumming the air—4, 3, 2, 1—and he was responding 4, 2, 3, 1. But then on one, he gave the rug a quick jab with this foot. Ah, he was suggesting the last of the repeated notes be quickly pedalled. What an idea! Joseffy certainly never hints at such an effect.

Mother looked delighted. She too jabbed the rug with her foot. No, he shook his head, *not quite fast enough*. He actually reached over and grasped her right leg above the knee, grasped the quadricep muscle and forced a quick tap of the imaginary sostenuto pedal. Now he was savoring the unheard sound. With his face tilted up in the lamplight,

19

I suddenly recognized him. At least I recognized a part of him. It was the nose of Frederick Chopin.

My mouth fell open. It was to gasp, I thought. But instead these words fell out, double *forte*, "Let's all go into the garden now." And I rotated—gracefully I could tell— to lead the way through the French doors. But why, when the chrysanthemums weren't ready?

The garden was ablaze in torchlight. Real torches, like the Statue of Liberty holds up, but with long handles planted in the ground, or jutting out from the back wall, torches like you see in some paintings of the garden of Gethsemane with that rich Dutch light flickering everywhere. And the chrysanthemums had been multiplied.

No longer just my neat mounds of red cushion mums. There was rank on rank of mums of all colors and forms. Spider mums in oranges and yellows. Giant football mums in purples, lavenders and whites, star-burst mums, fireballs and a thousand tiny button mums massed against the stucco wall. All the guests were gasping with delight. They hurried to stand among them, cupped individual blossoms like the chins of favored children; long index fingers pointed through the flickering light at flowers just beyond. When the guests knelt to study whole clumps, their bodies disappeared among the rows of flowers and their heads floated among them, heads themselves like large flowers or cabbages. Above us smiled the crescent moon.

I wanted to turn, to say *Mother, come look, come join us, they are so beautiful, thank you, thank you, they have never been so beautiful,* and of course I could not turn back. My body gasped with grief. The dreadful *rigor* seized me. Then all that was replaced with the turbulence and then the gaiety of the Chopin *Valse No. 14 in E Minor*.

Could I hold my breath throughout? Could I thus make the moment permanent? Could I make the air hold that music forever, vivid as a painting, more permanent than stone, sound becoming statuary of the air? And would the performance be perfect at last? Who played? Was it *he* or *she*?

I held my breath on and on as each passage of loveliness, the lightest, most gay of sounds, swept past. But where was the pedal touch on the fourth of the repeated notes? Of course it was withheld, withheld till the phrase was introduced for the last time, and then the pedal, a suggestion of poignant prolonging, a soupçon of romantic rubato, a wobble in rhythm, the human touch in the final offering of art. Then it ended.

Then, only then, the air rushed from my lungs. "BRAVO!" I shouted. Unbound, my jaw seemed to be permitted to open all the way to my heart. "HOORAY! HOORAY!" I shouted, raising my fist and punching the air over my head. All the guests shouted "BRAVO!" their fists aloft. And dozens of Roman candles, skyrockets, pinwheels shot up into the air, burst gloriously high above our heads, bloomed like flowers forced by a movie camera. I felt her standing behind me, her hand a warm squeeze on my elbow.

The next morning I found her note saying that she wanted to vacation in England. She had taken a morning flight. England because they spoke her language there. I walked into the bright garden. Of course, she had hired a clean-up crew to take away the spent torches and the mess. The gauzy crescent moon, the ghost of a thorn, hung in the blue.

I visited the rock. It had been rolled six feet west,

21

to the artistically correct place. The dark continent had returned to the bottom of the world, no longer visible at the juncture of rock and grass. The rock was right side up and mica glittered over its dome. Where it had stood gaped the chipmunk hole, wide enough for a human thigh. A dark, pleasant hole.

Ah, there was the chipmunk already, poising at the rim of damp earth, blinking in the sunlight.

Ice Skating
at the North Pole

I think that my husband is going to be unfaithful to me, and I don't know what to do about it. If it were not for our daughter, a little Viking with hair like braided sunshine, I would simply leave. When my first husband, Patrick, was unfaithful, we were childless. But Eric is the father of my daughter and the builder of our home.

"We'll have a house made of light," Eric said six years ago.

I bought the big woods. We stood on the limestone lip of a ravine, and he spread his hands. Rectangles of light cut themselves out of the air. He placed them upright, big panes four by eight feet, lined them up, with cherry beams between, and there was our house—a glass house, shaped like a shoebox, one end a wooden deck jutting over the ravine.

I won this man with magic hands by the special skill in my own hands. Indiana Old Settlers' Days. I saw him in the woods, lean as Abe Lincoln with the red hair of Thomas Jefferson. What forefathers we had! His costume was tailored impeccably. I pushed my sunbonnet back so he could see me well and stepped up to the pitching line. Horseshoe, boomerang. The rusty iron curved like a smile in my hand. Whispering U-U-U as it sailed through the air, the horseshoe ringed the stake and shimmied down to the grass.

"Good," someone murmured quietly.

I would have to do better than that.

I stepped back ten paces. Now my horseshoe was stainless steel, and I turned it like a mirror in my hand. Yes, I bounced the light into the corners of their eyes, made them look. Now I threw the horseshoe in a long arc, a ghost foot gliding up a hill of nothing and back down again to home, a lowly post.

"Ahhh," from many throats. As his head turned, light flashed back to me from the plane of the side of his nose.

I backed up again, lifting my pioneer skirt. I could feel the crowd parting behind me. One, two—twenty more steps I backed and opened the space between the stake and me. Way in the distance, the bare post rose up from the earth for me.

My arm like the pendulum of grandmother's clock, I swung from the shoulder—back, forth, back, forth and then let her sail. The horseshoe flew comet-like, with dust of many colors trailing in its wake.

And then his voice in my ear. "Aren't you the linguistics professor?" And our picnic in the woods.

We have lived in the woods ever since. Mature oaks and maples grow all around us. In autumn, as it is now, we are wrapped in tawny gold. We have no curtains on our glass walls, no other houses visible—just the enveloping woods.

The end of our house that sticks out in space is a deck with no railings. We have kept the sliding glass doors to the deck locked for four years, till our daughter has reached the age of reason. My rival is our daughter's kindergarten teacher.

Today we have invited Rosetta's whole class to come walk in our golden woods, and I have left the kitchen to stand on the deck, to see Eric guide them along our paths. Ms. Newsome's hair is black as a crow's wing. She wears a short red jacket. Eric holds out his hand, palm up, to help her over a log in the trail. Our daughter holds her other hand. Ms. Newsome's black head has the sheen of obsidian. And slices me. And I wonder what to do?

I look at my empty hands and into them, and I see my mother's bones. I have always had a special strength because I have always known that my own mother would do anything for me.

Had my mother's demonstration been less vivid, perhaps I would have taken more comfort from her loyalty. Eric looks for ideas to comfort me at night when I can't sleep. I haven't told him much about my mother because I do not wish to frighten him.

When I was a child, Mother—where was my father?—and I also lived in the woods, or were we just visiting there? Glacier National Park in a shiny trailer. Mother hated the encasement and kept the screenless trailer door open so we could look into the leaves, green as a color crayon. She was at the counter that was also our table. One end was bolted to the wall; the other end was curved carefully with no dangerous corners. Mother was cutting up a chicken. I remember the very stroke: she was holding the wing away from the plucked body, and the skin there stretched into a yellowish translucent web. The blade of the big butcher knife was poised above the V.

"Kitty," I said at the large soft face that hesitated for a moment in the open door. Its shoulders, big as sand dunes, moved, bunching themselves. My mother spun around with the knife in her hand. The cat stretched out long through the air, a sandy blur, and there was my mother's knife and her whole self in front of me. Mother and the mountain lion were rolling on the floor together, and it was snarling and shrieking. My mother was only grunting. The knife went up and down.

I was there in that rolling and twirling too, and with one claw the cougar opened my forearm from elbow to wrist. My blood was the reddest red. Nothing could ever be so vivid. I remember not screaming till I saw her face trying to smile at me, with bits of tan hair sticking to her chin.

There was a little newspaper article about us; I have it hidden some place: Trailer Mother Kills Cougar. I never showed the article to Patrick or even Eric—it's not well-written anyway. No vividness. The reporter hung back from the details as though he were incredulous, despite the evidence: the dead animal, our wounds, our pain in the hospital. But I named my daughter Rosetta, after Rose my mother.

After killing the cougar, my mother studied every situation for potential danger. Long before seat belts were standard, she had cleats bolted to the floor of our car and threaded with sturdy cotton belts. We were laced in like the tongues of two shoes. I am grateful for its convenience every time I buckle Rosetta's lap-and-shoulder harness, which she is only now tall enough to wear.

It is one of my secrets from everybody that Rosetta is not named just for my mother. She is also named for the Rosetta Stone. I loved the Rosetta Stone when I saw its picture in a children's encyclopedia. It gave me faith that languages wish to speak, they want to know each other. More than the people who utter them, perhaps. No one talks with me at our college, but then I am the only linguist at our small school.

"A small, *excellent* school," Eric always insists when I am gnawed by ambition and can't sleep. He has a vested interest in trying to associate Lincoln College with excellence, for he is the dean.

When the woman with black hair takes his hand in my woods, she is pleased that it is the dean's hand.

At night, as a last effort to calm me, Eric will say, "Well, Kathy, why don't you just get up and work on your book?" And, though I will be a wreck from sleeplessness the next day, I usually do.

My book is a revolutionary approach to grammar, we both believe. Its title is *A Grammar of Vividness*. I have known I would write it since I was ten years old. The insight that I had then is the one that drives me now. My fifth grade teacher was asking us to pick out the subjects of sentences. Do you remember how hard that was at first? "The pencil is red" was the sentence. Clearly, to me, the most important word in the sentence was and is *red*. *Red* is the instinctual subject. The entire utterance is for the word *red*.

"The bright horseshoe sails like a comet"—*bright* and *comet* are the poles of that utterance, because all the globe of that sentence spins between those words. "The bright horseshoe sails like a comet." Only a ninny, thousands of years of ninnies, would think that *horseshoe* and *sails* should be crowned subject and verb, lords of all they survey.

The music in prose and poetry is a matter of how the vividness is distributed, how the writer places the vividness in that time machine the sentence as it streams past. When I listen to William Carlos Williams read his own poetry, his theory of the variable foot comes clear. My analysis of his reading style is the chapter I'm working on. Then Roethke, then Dylan Thomas. I grew up with their voices, their recordings. These men, their voices have stayed with me, but one day my father kissed the scar on my arm and said goodbye to Rose and me forever.

My scar is a place other men have liked to kiss, whether they were saying hello or good-bye. Like onlookers drawn to a wreck, they come to place their lips there. Both my husbands, the lovers between them. It's as though they want its secret, the terrible knowledge I have that my mother would do anything for me. Probably if I had told them how she tore open the throat of the mountain lion, both Patrick and Eric would have called her heroic. The word is inaccurate.

Like a Chinese dragon, the children in their bright coats thread through the woods. Rosetta is proud to be at its head with her father, and so is Ms. Newsome. Their feet crackle in the thin gold leaves that clutter the path, and I turn away from the deck to the house. When the children come back from their walk, I will have hot baked beans ready.

Infidelity, unfaithfulness, husband, seduction, divorce—

the language of an outworn century, left over from my mother no doubt, but all I have to translate red pain. Years ago, I discovered Patrick's capacity for infidelity on a ship. We were plowing through the North Atlantic on our way to Ireland. It was scarcely my discovery: he practically shoved my face in it.

Our cabin had bunks, one atop the other. We had made love in the lower bunk, and then Patrick had climbed to the upper berth to sleep.

"Have you noticed the woman with the long hair?" he asked me. "The one with hair like a mare's tail?"

I pretended to be asleep. Hair like a mare's tail—and I could see her though I'd never seen her. It was where our languages met.

The next day in the ship's steel stairwell, she stopped me and introduced herself. "You must be Patrick's wife," she said. Her face was one of openness and sisterhood. I wondered how Patrick had described me so that she could recognize me. Tan hair? Bony neck? She held out her arm to have us shake hands, as two men might. A classy young woman. I saw she wanted no part of my Patrick's infatuation. When she went up the stairs, I turned to admire her long swatch of hair, the flat velvet bow at the nape of her neck, her white blouse and pleated skirt. She looked like a big girl, escaped from the high school where we worked. As the principal of Cloverdale High School, Patrick would never touch the girls there.

That afternoon on the ship, Patrick wanted to shoot trap off the fantail. He wasn't a very good shot.

"You try," he said, grinning.

I had never shot before. I was shocked when I exploded the first clay disk. The dun-colored particles floated in a little cloud for a moment. And then there was the next disk—equally easy to hit.

"Wow!" Patrick was saying, while I turned the third one into dust, a smudge against the blue sky.

He wanted me to keep shooting, but I had begun to tremble. Why had this power come to me, unless this were a moment of great need? Where was the need to be able to shoot anything I chose through the heart?

I thought of my mother and of the extraordinary abilities that lay in our bones, that could be called up, that were totally amoral. My mother would do anything for me, but she was instinctual, not heroic.

When I was six, she camped with me and two hundred other Brownies and their leaders and chaperones in a museum in Columbus. We had spread our sleeping bags among an exhibit of dinosaur skeletons. This was called a lock-in, a contained adventure.

She woke me in the middle of the night. "Kathy, don't make a sound," she said.

I tried to obey, but my nose made an involuntary sniff. The acrid odor of smoke? fire? hung in the air. She held her finger to her lips, stared into my eyes and then picked me up in my little sleeping bag. Soundlessly, she stepped across the sleeping girls. I looked back over her shoulder at them, thought about butterflies in their chrysalises. The night lights cast a lurid redness over them and up the tall bones of Tyrannosaurus Rex.

When we got to the front door, we saw that the woman who was the night guard was asleep. My mother carried me to our car, parked on the street.

Only when we were at home—she carried me in to the sofa—did I speak.

"Will they all burn up?"

"I don't know," she said.

I felt my lip tremble. I loved Mrs. Gray, our gentle troop leader.

"If we had wakened them," my mother said, "there would have been a panic. I couldn't have saved you."

I stayed awake all night, staring at the patch of ceiling above the sofa and waiting for it to redden. My mother sat beside me. When the morning newspaper thumped against the door at dawn, she brought it in and scanned the front page.

"No fire," she said and smiled comfortingly at me. "My mistake," she added.

When Mrs. Gray telephoned later that morning, my mother said that I had been sick in the night and she hadn't wanted to disturb anyone.

Mrs. Gray must have asked my mother why she hadn't left a note because my mother said, "Yes, I should have thought about that."

When it was time for the next Brownie meeting, I wouldn't go. I lay on the sofa and felt sorry. I never saw Mrs. Gray again.

But I remember that early special love that a girl can have for her teacher who is not her mother. Beside that knowledge, I place a picture of Rosetta looking up trustingly at Ms. Newsome last month in the amber woods, though we are between Thanksgiving and Christmas now, and all the trees have emptied their leaves.

Every night, Eric asks Rosetta how her day at kindergarten was, and did nice Ms. Newsome say anything funny today?

The stark trees remind me of dinosaurs surrounding

31

the house.

Rosetta's special strength seems to lie with words. She wrote a poem for Ms. Newsome that begins "The heart of the dinosaur looks like a cello." Eric is in love with the line, though he knows no other poetry. I look at their happiness in each other and freeze it in my mind. On the Rosetta Stone, were the hieroglyphics, the secret language of pictures, of direct vividness, betrayed by the other languages? What do my pictures mean if I refuse translation?

Patrick did not seduce the young woman with the mare's tail hair, but one day when I was in the tiny bathroom of our cabin, I heard the hall door swoosh open, and a heavy voice say "Sir!"

I went quickly into our bedroom, and there was an angry gray-haired man pointing a pistol at Patrick. "I'll blow a hole through your head if you ever touch my daughter again," he said, and then disappeared back into the hall.

Patrick was sitting in the upper berth, his legs hanging over the side.

"Patrick!" I gasped.

"Some madman," he said. "Lock the door and forget it."

The next day we docked. I had no idea which of the passengers was his daughter, or how young she was. I was young myself then. I never told any of our friends at Cloverdale High why I was divorcing Patrick, and he still lives in Ohio and is the principal there.

Then, as now, I have considered trying to take a tolerant attitude toward infidelity. I know how common it is, of course. But only the strictest fidelity excites me sexually; only it can replace the kind of loyalty that exists between mother and daughter.

By the time my mother died in an auto wreck, seat belts were standard, but hers was suspected of being defective. The insurance money and the manufacturer's check helped me get in and out of my marriage to Patrick and through school for two graduate degrees, was finally consumed in buying this land. I did not use *A Grammar of Vividness* for my dissertation. I knew it was too original for that.

How could my careful mother have failed to notice that the seat belt in her new car was defective? What was it that she swerved to miss that night on the deserted road that led to the zoo? I had been only a week in my new apartment at my new college. I was sitting on the sofa kissing Rodney, whom I had just met, when a policeman knocked at the door with the news.

Later I visited the leafy zoo road where Mother wrecked, and the insurance man asked if I thought she could have been startled in the dark, scared, by the picture on the billboard? It was a scene of big cats—a tiger, a panther, a leaping cougar.

"Not likely," I said, and I felt afraid.

He concluded she must have gone to sleep at the wheel. Though I have always known this could not have happened, I can conjure up a picture of her eyelids sliding down, her head bowing, the car curving toward the billboard. I will this sequence to be eternally vivid and true.

Today, we have our first snow of the year. Rosetta is snug in her kindergarten, but Eric cancelled all classes at our little college, which is atop some steep hills that we call the Knobs. The roads are dangerous just after a new snow.

"Let's walk in the woods," Eric suggests. He wants to take the shotgun and have me shoot it. "It's next week that I'll be away," he says. He doesn't want Rosetta and me to be alone in the country without a gun, he has decided. I think he has become a little paranoid because he is about to break our marriage vows. I think he will be with Ms. Newsome. I think she will call in sick one day and go to the capital to meet him. Of course I will know because I will ask Rosetta each day if anybody was absent.

"Let's walk to the pond and see if it's frozen," he says.

I put on my new red jacket and knitted black cap. We have good snow boots that almost reach our knees. This snow is already five inches deep, and the large flakes are still drifting down.

"'He will not see me stopping here / To watch his woods fill up with snow,'" I quote.

"Who?" Eric asks. His degree was in business. "It's ⌐ your woods."

"Your house, my land," I say.

"Kathy," he puts his arm across my shoulders. "Don't be morose."

"Maybe I'd better seize the day to work on my book."

He stops squeezing me and picks up the shotgun. "The walk will clear the cobwebs out of your brain."

He is wonderfully handsome. Lean and square-jawed, in contemporary clothes Eric looks like a fashion model. No wonder the Board of the college love for him to represent them. I tag along after him.

The woods are lovely, and I am close to saying so, but only mutter "'dark and deep.'"

He stops on the trail. Our house juts out behind

34

and above us. Snow is piling up on the open deck.

"Kathy," he looks at me squarely in the eye. "Don't mutter."

"Why not?"

"Well, if you want to know. People at school think you're acting strange. Of course you don't need to worry—"

"—since you're the dean," I finish for him.

He sighs. "See, this is where you put the shells in." He slides four shells into the magazine, depressing a metal door. I don't listen. I remember how I slid open the glass door letting little Rosetta step onto the deck for the first time. Finally, he swings the gun up to his shoulder and fires at a tree ten yards down the path. The shot tears away a patch of bark on the side of the tree. The sound rings through the white woods and hills. He slams the wooden pump up and down and says, "See if you can shoot anything."

I hit the same tree, dead center.

"Great!" he exclaims, and suddenly I remember how Patrick shouted *Wow!* on the fantail of the ship, how the gray-haired man came to our cabin and pointed his finger, so like a pistol that it was a pistol, at Patrick.

"Cock it again," I say. This time I watch how he does it.

"Aim farther away," he instructs.

"See the birch?" I ask as I aim. It is thirty yards down the path.

I bam it.

"See the pine cone?" I quickly jerk the slide, which is so stiff it hurts my arm to make it move. The pine cone is silhouetted against the sky, hanging like a Christmas ornament many feet beyond the birch. I blast it into next year.

"Hey, Annie Oakley!" he says. "What do you mean, you don't know how to shoot?"

"Somebody has to set up the situation for me," I say. I am pleased with my power.

Eric and I decide not to walk to the pond. We go back to our house and make love on the living room rug. His hands rub me as though I were a magic lamp.

Afterward, I sit naked on the sofa and stare out the glass wall into the black trees and white hills. I see a crow. I think, why I could shoot it, if I stood on the deck. I think of the bird's toppling out of the sky. It might fall on someone passing below on the path, on Carol Newsome. Its wings, like dark hair, hang down beside her pink cheeks.

All this week, each day while Eric is gone, I ask Rosetta if everyone is well at school.

Rosetta and I are eating hot tomato soup at a little oval table with carved, bowed legs and a marble top. The table is beside a glass wall, and all outdoors is there for us to see. We are admiring the birds flying like something out of Breughel through the snowy woods.

Today Rosetta says, "We are all there, but Ms. Newsome is out with sniffles." In the same breath—does Rosetta know to change the picture?—she says, "Please, can't we go to the pond? Can't we skate?" Her fingers make skating motions on the marble.

I am shocked at the recklessness of her question. I see ice going soft under her small foot. First the blade only sinks a little deeper, and she is fascinated by the water slushing over the white toe of her boot. The freezing water rises to her ankle, but the laces tightly binding down the tongue have made a good seal and her foot is still dry.

36

When the hole opens up like a black mouth she is suddenly up to her knees in it and sinking, flinging her arms up for me to save her.

I erase the scene, smile across the marble table at her. For a moment I think that I will show her the cougar skin. I will turn the tan fur to the floor, lay her on the red felt lining and wrap her in it. She will be safe as a child swaddled in a good marriage. But the skin is too well hidden to find.

"Sure," I say and smile at Rosetta. "Let's get our skates and wraps."

We walk out into the snow and down the path away from the house. It is too cold to be out like this. The wind cuts through the black trees. When we can no longer see the house I know that I am taking her north, all the way north by dog sled.

We travel for many days. The feet of the dogs are bleeding.

Finally, the needle of my compass strains to point straight down.

Here there is never wind. At our feet, the wind has blown the ice clear of snow, a perfect lens. Like the eye of a hurricane, this place is the eye of the world.

"Here's where we'll skate," I say. I hold up our glittering skates. The aurora borealis springs from the blades. As I kneel and bow my head to lace our boots, I know this ice is a mile thick, has never been known to thaw.

Essence for Ms. Venus

After the corn was cut in Iowa, when the game was fat, I stopped at a provincial courthouse to get my hunting license. I signed the license *Diana* and shoved the form across the golden oak casement to the clerk.

"You'll have to put down both names, Miss," she said.

"In some locales," I replied, "for some personages, a single name is sufficient. For poets."

"What name?"

"Homer, for example."

She quickly inscribed *H* in the blank space.

"Wait," I said. "Not Homer. *Hunter.*"

"Even poets got last names here," she said. She lifted her eyes and nodded toward the open window at my back.

Through the courthouse window, in the distance, I saw hordes of brightly dressed college students jostling each other on the sidewalks of the town. As though every student were a poet.

The clerk frowned to see me take my traveler's check from a quiver instead of from a purse. Inside the quiver, my knuckles brushed the rough leather, then a small, empty flask, a reminder to take cousin Venus a bottle of perfume. (The impedimenta one is asked to cart home; it's enough to make one think twice about traveling.) The clerk laid out the stamps for the license.

While I signed the traveler's check, my eye was distracted by the beauty of their duck stamps—tinted Aegean blue and the green of olives—and my ear by a divorce proceedings down the hall. I heard certain words, thundered in a legal male voice: "And it is your firm belief, is it not, that, as stated in your joint petition for divorce, the marriage is irretrievably broken?"

"Now, your husband's not allowed to hunt on your license," the clerk chirped in my other ear.

I stooped to tie my sandal.

"I have no use for husbands."

Irretrievably broken? Hearts are irretrievably broken, but not legal contracts. Maybe modern hearts are tougher—made of molded vinyl.

Yes, I would investigate their sense of *broken.*

Why marry, indeed, but why, having done it, divorce? A million reasons, of course. Of all the reasons, the one that offends me most is a lack of chastity in marriage. Adultery, to put the Hebrew slant on it.

I strode toward the courtroom—a janitor left swabbing the marble floor to gawk at my stature—and I entered, at the rear.

Their courtroom was empty except for the essential configuration:

The bald judge in his black robes sat round as a pumpkin, with his head bent.

The woman with her oval face blank, frightened, staring unseeing, was facing me. A long softly-braided rope

40

of brown hair hung over her shoulder, lay in loops in her lap. She was thin and had no bosom to speak of.

Her lawyer, a scrawny, nervous type from Legal Aid, asked the necessary questions.

The fourth and last person present was the woman's witness, a friend mythologized for the occasion into middle-class innocuousness; she wore a tan wrap skirt and a nearly matching beige summer pullover.

His presence not being essential, the husband was absent from the amicable proceedings. Off hunting, perhaps, as I should be.

"Mitch wanted other women."

Wanted? Immaterial, I'd say. Behavior—that's the question. I've never held with the Christian ethic that what you do in your heart is as bad as done, *fait accompli*. What is chastity but a bright girdle for the physical being? But I have no quarrel with the imagination, the light of the moon, the fragrance of perfume, with wanting.

"Are you saying your husband was unfaithful to you?"

"Yes."

Her face was turned up; she was seeing Mitch. Probably he was ugly as a toad, but the lost and shining one for her.

She was wearing a dress she'd made herself—the princess style, seams curved to maximize bosom. The fabric background was neutral as skin and the cloth was coarsely woven in imitation of homespun. It was printed all over with flowers of the gayest hues—red daisies, yellow snapdragons, blue cornflowers with all sorts of unlikely green leaves and vinery twining around. Anyone could see that she'd chosen the fabric to remind herself of Botticelli's *Primavera*. But spring was past now; it was hot midsummer, and later. It was the hunting season.

When the stag turns for the marsh, when his heart-shaped hooves suck out of the spongy earth, when the hound is at his short-haired flank, then I slip the arrow to the string, draw the feathers to my ear.

"How often was he unfaithful?"

"Repeatedly."

She bowed her head; the part of her hair shone like a scar.

A gang of men I passed in the country had been haying with an old, overshot haystacker, and I saw again the great ropes that dangled from the haystacker, and then the woman's braid of brown hair. How many unfaithful among them? At this hour, those men, fraternal as a legal club, would be peacefully sitting in the shade of the stack, lounging, drinking sun-tea from quart jars. One of the ropes moves slightly in the hot air. Their draft horses are standing apart in the sun rubbing their bowed necks together, stamping flies off their fetlocks.

The young lawyer fussed in his notes; he seemed to have forgotten the next question. The judge's massive head slowly swung toward her. His voice croaked up from a frog-belly throat.

"And did you object to this behavior?"

She turned to him, forgot her ritual lines, confessed.

"I tried not to. He believed it was *natural*. With Mitch it was many women. I couldn't help it. I was jealous. After Easter, when he told me about having them, he said he wasn't going to stop. He said he wasn't going to sneak around anymore either. But I was jealous. He said I was going to have to choose. If I couldn't take it, we'd have to divorce."

42

I am transfixed by her quiet and intense speaking. Inexplicably, I envy her her pain. Like the moment when the arrow enters the hind, her moment is sternly real. And that past moment of revelation—Mitch would have taken her to some natural grove, a circle of hickory trees clustered like a gazebo above a pond, a grove frequented by the hare, the dove and the lecherous sparrow, a grove where wood-hyacinth pushed through the leafmold. A natural setting for an instinctual ultimatum. *It* was real in my imagination, too. Past them thunders a herd of wild rams, which I will hunt, kill.

From the black robes, judgment intoned. "Do you have further questions, Mr. Jones?" The judge's face, pale as the underside of a harvest-ripe vegetable, revolved toward her. His mouth opened like a strange navel. "Speaking of the natural, *wolves* mate for life, my dear."

She was dismissed, dazed again, from the witness chair, and her friend replaced her.

Her friend understood these proceedings perfectly. Her voice was beige. The point had been made, she wished only to echo; she knew the decorum of a divorce, probably had helped more than just this time. She swore that she had known the couple for a year, saw them struggle for reconciliation. I knew that she had known the woman two months, had never seen the man. As a witness, she was perfect.

The judge granted the divorce, stated that the man ought to pay the court costs, $12.50. But of course he was in Texas, in bed with his redheaded lover.

I leave the room, hurry through a marble-paved hallway and down the granite steps. In the distance, collegiate men mill on the sidewalks of the town, forget the farms they left, the cylindrical corncribs, the countryside crossed with game. On the green around the courthouse, two young professionals—lawyers, doctors, consuls—play frisbee in their white shirt sleeves. The noon hour, almost— time for a little boyish recreation before growing portly, wearing black robes, knowing they know.

As their red disk flashes through the air, I snap my fingers and my hound lunges for it.

A cross-bred greyhound, his muscles are like nothing they have ever seen. His teeth are triangular, the jaw is a wedge, his heritage from a shark. His white teeth close on the frisbee in mid-air, between the men. One of them approaches him—"Here dog, give it to me." My hound slings their toy from side to side; beneath his hide all his muscles squirm in excess of power; he puts his paw in their vinyl saucer, lifts his head and holds up a jagged, torn-off half for me to see. Their frisbee irretrievably broken.

Good dog.

The guardians of the law run down the browning courthouse lawn.

I hide behind a myrtle bush. Here comes Selena, broken-hearted, and her wise friend Fortuna, her beige voice turned autumnal gold.

"If he gets us the new house, the one with the indoor swimming pool . . . I'll stay." (Chastity, I wonder, or a slave's bargain.)

Selena's face shines blankly as a silver coin, round and valueless. Her brains have been sucked out Egyptian style, through the nostrils, her eyes replaced with ornamental glass.

Their lawyer passes them, mounts his bicycle to hurry

44

inexpensively back to Legal Aid. The big-footed judge paddles down the walkway from a side door to his limousine. They are pleased with their civilized hearing, the modest cost. They are content with so little suffering—so little justice. Those spinning feet, their mechanical justice—all can be changed and hunted.

Yet, my neat, small points are for the hare rushing under the blackberries and for the ring-neck pheasant whirring out of dry grass. And beyond the field is the forest where the rumps of deer brush past pale birch, and my big bow is tuned to two-hundred pounds of pull. I let the mortals go.

I lift my eyes to the pale sky. The cloudy ghost of a full moon floats there. Behind me, their ridiculous courthouse, a solid rectangle of red sandstone with a superfluous square spire rising above the county and the nothing of a town.

I reach in my quiver, rummage among the broadheads. Here is that round perfume bottle, blown from milky glass. Translucent here, clear there, thick-sided. Heavy enough for a throwing stone, well able to break through bone, if I should choose to hunt that way. If I should choose to hurl it to Texas.

I open its glass stopper. All of the perfume of this trivial, provincial place—where they claim the hunting is worth a trip—flows into the bottle. Its milky sides are streaked with blood.

I will seek my doe-eyed cousin in the woods. Let her sniff this essence. Essence of Human Intercourse—her specialty. What do I know about it? And what name have they given her now? Not Aphrodite, or Venus. Something more modern? Vinita? Vinnie?

Perplexed, I touch my face. Like ripened fruit, like

the moon, I have two cheeks. Is it time to turn the other cheek? The dark-sided one? Here, where the bow has twanged and snapped and thwarped for years, the flesh has grown slick and hard. Black and tough as shoe leather. It has an odor now. It smells . . . unchaste, ravenous, promiscuous.

On First Hearing
Artful Singing

No one can predict what will be the difficult part in the final breakup, in a divorce. Dividing the books and records was an unexpected difficulty. What I had not foreseen was that in giving up Nick, I would give up his past. His childhood, his youth would become as inaccessible to me as the material possessions he packed off in cardboard boxes begged from the liquor store.

Before we were married, when Nick lent me *The Magic Mountain* and *Remembrance of Things Past*, I read them only to know how Nick's consciousness had leaned eagerly forward here, stopped to meditate there, glimpsed visions of the perfect. Fischer-Diskau, he'd say, Hermann Prey, as he turned on the stereo: *Kindertotenlieder*, *Schwannengesang*. And the world of art song whorled in my ears. What I had wanted to know before we married: what mind was his to be so moved by their vision, by their singing?

What I want to know twelve years after my divorce:

47

why his past is small change in my hand, coins I continually thumb as they become smooth, blank and silent.

1

Nick is five and he is sitting on the curb: he has been forbidden by his mother to cross the street to smell the lilacs that grow on the other side. He is tiny, his large nose is lifted, sniffing, sniffing, sucking the purple across the street. His clothes are gray-striped like the ticking for a feather pillow. Lilac, odor of lilacs, pours across the concrete, rushes like a cataract through the blackness of his nostrils.

2

Still very young, Nick is standing beside a pussy willow shrub. He caresses the gray nodes, he traces them up the branches. He picks a node and rolls it between his finger and thumb. The hard pellet within the fuzz teases him. He slips the pussy willow into his nose, stuffs it far up with his finger.

She goes after it with tweezers, a bright bill extending from that bird, her hand.

3

An adolescent, Nick dreams of the West, the desert, but it is the Civil War where his father rides in gray. His father is the only upright thing in the landscape of lavender and pink horizontals. Cradled in the sights of Nick's rifle, his father's image is small. Nick awakens smiling.

4

When I am a graduate student in Minnesota, he comes to my apartment that first winter wearing his father's duck-hunting coat. It is enormous and he loves it. The coat is gray, filled with goosefeathers, and he says you can never feel cold in such a coat, but he leaves his hands out in the weather. He lets himself in with the key I have given him, and he wakes me by placing his frozen hands on my belly.

5

We are married quickly, and when we visit his parents for Thanksgiving, his mother asks me if I would like to have Tay's old dress shoes, bought last summer in Paris. The shoes are size seven and surely she can see that my feet are at least size nine.

On the way home, Nick tells me that when he was three, they found him trying to smother the infant Tay with a pillow. Even at three, he knew that his mother preferred Tay. Nick tells me that he used to adore his mother anyway, used to speak inwardly in her voice, used to bring her briar roses in the spring. Just before presenting the roses he squeezed their stems. When he opened his palm she saw dots of blood, exclaimed that he was hurt.

When he presented me to her, I noticed that he

49

opened his hand, showed her his palm.

6

Even after we are married, I imagine his adolescent body: he is dressed in black tights, he wears something on his head to protect his ears, he is down on all fours wrestling with some other boy who does not love music or read *The Interpretation of Dreams* or say *Descartes, Nietzsche, Wittgenstein*. I feel sorry for Nick, hate his kneeling on the mat straining with the other.

He says to me: *I won't hurt you; let me just show you; hold still; put your arm behind your back while I—* And always he twists until I cry out.

7

When Nick is depressed in the summer, at night, I suggest that we leave Wittgenstein on the kitchen table, that we take a walk to see the lightning bugs. The bugs hover only two blocks from our apartment; there is a dip, a wide black pocket where they stay. It is like a view of fairyland to see the thousands of them floating and winking there. It is as though we are in an airplane on a night flight looking down at some fragile city.

He tells me how they remind him of when he was a boy—I have that memory, though now I do not know what comes before or after it—a boy in North Carolina, and how, when he was lonely, he went down to their pond. The bugs hovered above the water there, and the sky was

50

black enough to see the Milky Way. He watched till he could hardly tell whether he was looking at stars or lightning bugs. He stood on the shore so long that his ankles sank into the ooze. He says that he was always aware of his mother's kitchen window while he stood beside the pond, aware of a shapeless glowing from up on the hill.

We walk into the black pocket to be among the lightning bugs, and pretending to be a dog, Nick snaps at them.

On the way home, Nick names the houses, "Bourgeois Splendor," "Bourgeois Magnificence." He compares them to the grand houses in the country and in the city his family has lived in. He wonders if we will ever live in such a house, and I tell him it doesn't matter. He wonders if he will ever finish the paper on Wittgenstein, already two weeks overdue, if he will ever finish his degree.

That night, when I am asleep, he shoves me out of bed, when he was asleep, too, he says.

8

Our last Christmas together, we visit my mother, and Nick stands beside her piano and sings Schubert. She has played these songs before, years ago in her youth. He politely asks her to speed up the tempo; his thumb and forefinger closed in a circle, he conducts a little to show her. She nods, is pleased. I sit on the sofa and embroider a cherry tree as a cover for a pincushion. It is a design from the Federalist period, and the cherries are composed of a cluster of French knots. I make the knots beautifully. Firm, round and minute, the French knots stand up on the linen.

Later, he tells me that his father once bought his mother a Steinway grand and had it placed in the living room. He told her to learn to play, but she never did. While we are at my mother's house, Nick will not touch me after we go to bed.

*

I am married now to a man whose past was one of poverty and parental cruelty. His mother put him next to a garbage can behind a restaurant in Omaha to find his supper; his father blinded him in one eye. It is a past that is too flamboyant to entice me. A calm, good man, my husband cooks soufflés for me, reminds me to have my teeth cleaned, baits my fishhook with three kernels of corn.

I am ordinary, like Nick, and it is the puzzle of small moments—lilac and pussy willow, the tip of a thorn just under the skin, the sound of a key turning in a lock, the way a bright needle pierces linen—whose essence draws me back.

I press my finger again on the same rosy French knots. They speak like braille.

I remember our happiness, how I loved to hear his artful singing.

The Woman Who Knocked Down Walls

Tennessee

Their children had odd names. A week after the first one was born, their house had caught on fire. She had been at home alone, and she had rescued the baby and the dog and cat and even pulled the sofa out into the yard before people held her and thrust the baby into her arms and told her she had to be careful of herself for *his* sake. At the time of his birth, they hadn't been able to agree on the right name for their first child, but after the fire, they decided to call him Blaze.

When the second baby was born, he had six signs, six marks on his body that the doctors had pointed to.

"That baby's *not* retarded," the woman said to her husband. She said it from her hospital bed, only four hours after delivery, she said it not even holding the baby, alone, just looking up from the wrinkled hospital sheets, she wrinkling her forehead only slightly as she said what had to be true to her husband. "I don't care about the crease in his hand," she went on. "I've looked at him, I've looked in his eyes, and I know that baby's got just as much sense as you or me."

When the man came back later to see his wife, she, holding the baby in her arms, looked over its sparse dark hair with perfect triumph: "See, he's sucking. They thought he couldn't." And she looked more confident, more pulled-together than she had after Blaze was born. They agreed to call this one Fallow, for the earth, and for what they were going to accomplish with him.

She bought twenty alarm clocks as soon as they went home from the hospital. Each one was set to go off at a different time, and there was a card under each one saying what she should do at that moment with the baby. Starting at four A.M., she played peek-a-boo for five minutes. At five, she rubbed his rattle into his hand. At six, she played buzzing bees into his stomach to make him laugh. And on it went. She taught her husband the games, and he began to make up games too, which he performed on the half-hour.

Once she went to visit a state nursery for the retarded to find out if they were doing things she didn't know about, but what she found was that all the babies needed changing, and when she ordered the attendants to get out the fresh diapers, and when they wouldn't, she grabbed the diapers out of the linen closet and started on the baby in the first crib, and went all the way down the ward changing every baby. She told her husband she'd never seen such pitiful little red bottoms in all of her life, and he wrote a letter to the governor for her because they both agreed that he was

54

best at that kind of thing, and together they would get things done.

After five months she took Fallow back to the doctors and they said, yes, it was true, there weren't any signs anymore, but it was because they had made a mistake the first time and not because of anything she might have done, because that was impossible. Three of the men sat close around her telling her this, their knees almost rubbing against hers, and one of them with a sharp black beard, and all of them in their long white coats, with the starched sashes untied and dangling down to the floor. "Well," she said, "I just think that you all don't know as much as you all think you know," but she smiled at them when she said it because she had been a beauty queen in college before she had quit, pregnant, to marry the man who was not handsome but who composed love songs about her and played the guitar and whose family had money on top of that which made him all right with her sorority sisters. They said he had charm.

The doctors all laughed when she criticized them, and they all bent forward at the same time, and they all clapped their hands on their knees, and then they all stood up, and the smartest one with the bright black beard walked down the hall with her, looked up at her because she was five-foot-ten and said that it wasn't common to make that sort of diagnostic error, and, of course, they were always *glad* when it did turn out to be a mistake on their part, but that she really ought to let them do a genetic analysis, which would only take about a month, and then she could feel really sure.

She said, "I'm already sure," and then she passed through the revolving door into the sunshine.

55

Her husband said it was just another example of incompetence, and he was fed up with the incompetence of the South, and he wanted to leave his graduate program at the University, which was also a seedbed of incompetence, and leave the whole Southern system which wasn't good for her either and go to the Midwest and study with a man who had had to leave Germany because of Hitler and who was a friend of Einstein. And they left Tennessee and moved to Iowa.

Iowa

The first year they lived in an apartment in Iowa City. She stayed there all day working with the two babies, and he stayed at the University, and sometimes he brought new people home for her to meet because she needed to grow, too. But she didn't much like these people: they were communists and they talked about their hatred of the United States Government and how the war in Viet Nam was a war of genocide.

Sometimes these men were married and their wives came too, and she showed one of them her clippings from the Miss Tennessee contest, and the woman seemed interested and said that her whole family had watched the Miss America pageant on TV when she was little, and she had seen Miss Mississippi get it two years in a row, which nobody thought was fair.

Matt didn't like living in town. He said that when they had talked about moving to the Midwest that what he had really visualized was an Iowa farm. She understood.

He wrote to his father, then talked long-distance to

56

him several times. Matt's father insisted on talking to her, too, for a few minutes, to say that she'd always be *his* Beauty Queen. She said she'd gotten so big now, pregnant again, that she needed a nice big old farmhouse herself, and Matt could go hunting on his own property anytime without having to get up any partner. Even before they left town, Matt bought two big black dogs and they named them Bo and Selma. So they moved to the farmhouse and Matt killed a deer in an old cornfield the second day. They decided to butcher it themselves. She read a book that showed how and did as much of the cutting as Matt. She liked seeing how the animal was built in layers and systems, felt that doing this prepared her for something.

Her grandmother came up from Tennessee to stay with them. Patience was a farm woman herself, and she shook her head sadly to see what they had bought. "This house will be the devil-to-pay to heat," the old woman said. "You're likely to burn it down like you did in Tennessee."

"I didn't burn it down," Debbie said, but she liked the wild way of her grandmother's teasing.

When the contractions started and they were driving north to the University Hospital, she looked at the steps of all the farmhouses that they passed, and thought that none were as pretty as they should be.

This baby was a girl, and all the doctors agreed that she was a perfect specimen of good health. She wondered if Matt had told them that they better not say anything bad about this baby: they were that enthusiastic. They wanted her to put the baby on an experimental diet (all free food), but Debbie actually shouted, "Nuts to that. All my babies start on mother's milk."

57

She felt wonderful; it was such a relief to have a baby that everyone agreed was healthy and beautiful. When people from the philosophy department came with Matt to the hospital, she couldn't help gloating a little. "Isn't she a winner?" she said to them.

As she carried the baby up the steps of the farmhouse, she almost caught her toe in a rotten board. At supper she told Matt, "Those steps are coming out." He had agreed in a way that meant that he wasn't paying any attention.

Ten days later she went down to the basement and found a crowbar. The basement was horrible. Matt had locked the hunting dogs down there for three days while they were gone to the hospital and they had defecated all over the place. Matt had been too busy to clean it up. As soon as she had gotten home she had thought that there was a bad odor all over the house but she had gotten used to it. But here it was in the basement—old dog-do just everywhere. She took the crowbar out of the coalpile and then went around to the front of the house.

Just as she suspected, it was easy. She put the tip of the crowbar in a rotten spot and pried up the board. The wood made a wonderful straining sound. On the stubborn places she first tried working the crowbar up and down like a pump handle; then she braced the crowbar across her pelvis, held on with both hands, her wrists close together and brought her weight to bear on it.

Matt heard the noise and came down from his study. He picked up the crowbar and started smashing up the boards much faster than she had been able to.

"You're supposed to be studying!" she said.

"You go read philosophy," he said. "This is more fun."

58

"Let me help," she said. "I'll get the claw-hammer."

"GRRR," he said. "Give me a place to stand and a lever, and I'll move the whole universe." A rotten board jumped out with a long rusty nail dangling helplessly at its end.

It wasn't that there weren't some happy times on the farm, like the day they started in on the steps, but it was terribly isolated. Matt had to go into town to take classes and to teach some classes. She thought about him often during the day and would tell the children while she fed them what she thought he might be doing. They made it into a kind of game—she and Blaze, who could talk some now. He was her favorite child, though each was special in a special way—Fallow because she had saved him (she was sure that she had), and Windy was special because she was the only girl. But Blaze could talk.

"What's he doing now, Blaze?"

"Reading," Blaze pronounced very slowly.

"That's right!" she would exclaim. "Reading, and then teaching. Now listen, Blaze. What does Daddy study?"

She had been over this before, but Blaze still went blank at this question. His forehead looked like a little furrowed field. He could tell it was important; Debbie planned to surprise Matt some day like this. She watched Blaze carefully, and just before his frustration broke into tears she said very cheerfully: "Phi - LOS - O - phy."

"Los," Blaze said quietly and looked down.

In a way, she thought, working with beauty pageants had prepared her for this because enthusiasm was so important there, too. But this was better, she thought, taking a bite of apricot, because it really meant something to the children; it helped them. The judges knew surely that some of it was just a put-on.

And she had learned from the pageants how to handle the special kind of fatigue that came from being enthusiastic for other people all day. When you feel *drained*, then you must never hesitate. Whatever occurs to you that you *could* do or say, you *must* do. She thought about a kung-fu demonstration that she had seen on TV once. The man had said it was very important to shout while you attacked someone—that made your whole body go on alert. Well, you had to deliver a silent shout to your whole system when you were *drained*. As soon as you thought of something—like PICK UP THE DIRTY DISHES when you were comfortable at the table about to open a magazine—then next you had to DO IT. Now she looked at the dirty dishes.

PICK UP THE DIRTY DISHES. She even said it under her breath this time.

"I can't," Blaze said.

"I know, baby," she said, and kissed him. This time she was careful not to mutter—the idea!—PICK UP THE DISHES. But her body didn't move. Instead she thought of the word *drained*.

Although she had to get up to do it, she went over to the magnetic memo pad on the refrigerator and tore off a small sheet. Then she sat down again. She actually let her body plop down. Suddenly that was scary. She NEVER let herself flop around. Never. But she had been about to try to write something. Maybe that was part of it.

Bone tired, she wrote. Then she started a new line.
Yesterday I was full of energy.
I smiled like girls in new magazines.
Today, I'm DRAINED.

60

That was the point that she wanted to make, and she felt better about things. She could add more—maybe something about the muddy paw prints on the door glass. She had been letting them slide. The glass was a solid brown smear now. Maybe Matt would wash it off. Bo and Selma were his dogs. She remembered how after they had finished tearing out the steps that day, Matt had gone back upstairs to his study, and she had gone down to the basement to shovel up the dog-do. She had put it in two large grocery bags. As she carried it up the basement stairs, she had had a horror that a bag would burst, and that it would go all over the stairs, and she'd have to clean it up again. If that had happened it would have been like something inside *her* had burst, and she wouldn't have been able to stand it.

She focused on the little magnetic ladybug memo holder. OH, PICK UP THE DISHES she told herself. She got up and started stacking up the cereal bowls. Then she glared at the refrigerator. She didn't like that ladybug. She went over and plucked it off the side of the refrigerator like picking a tick off one of the dogs. She threw it in the garbage.

Then she looked around, surprised to see, why, there were the children. And they'd been with her all this time when she wasn't thinking of them or Matt at all.

When Matt came home that evening, as soon as she got the chance, she said, "You know, I think I had a philosophical experience this afternoon." Then she explained that her mind had told her body to do something and it hadn't done it.

"I guess your will wasn't really engaged," he said. "I mean, in some sense, your body knew that your mind was talking big but that it didn't mean it."

61

"I was thinking that maybe that it was a little related to that problem you told me about—the mind and body problem."

"The mind-body problem. Yes, in a way it is. What was it that your body wouldn't do?"

She was embarrassed and she had to laugh before she could say, "Pick up the dirty dishes."

That night in their bedroom, they talked and Matt said that she ought to have more activities to occupy her mind, or some projects. She recited her poem, and he said that he would try to do more to help her, and maybe she should talk to some of the people at the University about writing poems. She said that she didn't feel that she was ready for that but that she had a project in mind—to enlarge the size of the living room. Especially now that they had furniture, it seemed cramped. Not the kind of spacious farmhouse she had pictured when they decided to move to the country. He said for her to have a free hand.

"Matt," she asked, "do you think much of me and the children while you're away?"

"No," he said, surprised. "I never think of you at all."

She had thought he would say yes and that that would be the end of the thought. Instead it was like she was wading and stepped into something deeper, cooler, than she had expected. Then she remembered how for a moment that very day she herself had been surprised to look around and see the children and they had even been right there with her all along.

"Aw, honey," he said into her silence. He put his arm around her.

"Oh, I'm O.K.," she said and was surprised at how

long it took to get the brightness into her voice. She really did feel O.K., though. Yes, she liked for him to tell the truth; it was something she had always respected about him.

"I think of you a lot, though," she added.

He started to play to her, but she fell asleep in the middle of the song.

Each day as she saw the last of Matt's truck puff down the dirt road, she took the key and unlocked the windowseat where she kept the mattock. This way she didn't have to go to the basement, which still smelt bad, or if the weather was bad, she didn't have to get wet going to the barn. With the padlock, as long as she never forgot to lock it, all the dangerous tools were safe from the children in the convenient windowseat. She never would forget to lock it—of this she was absolutely sure. She wouldn't have let herself keep the tools there if she weren't certain.

What were the will, will power, confidence? What if her mind became defective and she forgot and Blaze managed to lift up the mattock and drop it on his foot? Suppose he became crippled because she falsely trusted herself? She had these thoughts just to entertain herself. If there was one thing she was absolutely sure of, it was that she was not going to cripple her children.

Before she took out the mattock, she checked that the children were confined in the old-fashioned entry hall, closed in like lambs in a little pen by two baby gates. She fastened each gate with a strong snaplock, so stiff that it turned her knuckles white to press it in.

She unlocked the windowseat and took out the mattock. A double door joined the living room and the dining room. It was her idea to make it one large room. To

63

remove the walls on both sides of the double door.

She raised the mattock over her head. She ran toward the wall, stopping her body a yard before it, now bringing the mattock up over her head, not breaking the momentum of her charge. AUGGGH she yelled as the mattock blade bit into the plaster. Sometimes it stuck there, and she had to wrench it loose. Other times it skittered off the hard plaster and slid down the wall to bounce on the floor. Debbie kept very careful account of where her feet were; she instantly judged what was going to happen and her body sprang away very quickly to avoid any injury.

She had worked with the children on this so that they wouldn't be frightened. At first she had sat on the floor with them and said Augggh to them in a soft way, and got them to say it afterward. Gradually she had increased her volume. She stationed them in the entry hall while she simply walked around the living room and occasionally said Augggh. Then she galloped around the living room. Finally she could run full tilt toward the wall, draw up short of it, and yell AUGGGH!

The children loved it. She knew it was important for them to have noisy exercises as well as intellectual ones.

Next, she accustomed them to the sound of her tool striking. She started with a little stick that she tapped lightly against the bars of Fallow's playpen. Then she took the mop handle and tapped the wall with it. She coordinated the sound of AUGGGH with the moment the mop handle hit the wall. First she did this in the entry hall with the children and quickly turned to kiss each of them just as soon as she had made the big bang.

When she moved to the living room, which was where she intended to knock down the wall, she couldn't

64

kiss them but she looked at them quickly and gave a big smile. It was rather like being in a pageant. She had never stumbled but she knew what she would have done if she had. As soon as the clumsy motion was over, she would turn to the judges, look them straight in the eyes, sparkle, smile, and think I LOVE YOU as loudly as she could while she held her smile.

But soon the children knew that she was supposed to hit the wall. So now it was perfect. She stood in front of the windowseat, the starting line. She raised the mattock over her head. She ran toward the wall, stopping her body a yard before it, now bringing the mattock up over her head, not breaking the momentum of her charge. AUGGGH she yelled, AUGGGH the children yelled, her cheering section, AUGGGH she yelled as the mattock blade bit into the plaster. Instantly, her body, like a trustworthy mind, judged what was going to happen and she took care of herself so that there was no possibility of injury. That wouldn't be fair to the children if she let herself get hurt.

The broken plaster was like chips and hunks of bone, only some pieces had a thin film of green paint on their flat side. She always swept the plaster up so that the living room would be relatively neat when Matt got home. Still it was hard to control the plaster dust. It was like the odor from the basement. Before long it was all over the house, and when Matt wanted to sing in bed, he often had to wipe plaster dust off the face of his guitar. He didn't care though. Every day he admired the progress she had made.

Soon she didn't have to stop after each blow to smile at the children. She just slung the mattock into her arm like a man would carry a shotgun, except reversed, with the head up, like a woman would cradle a child and walked across the room to her starting point. She charged the wall till she was red all over, sweating, coated with plaster dust, huffing for breath. When she huffed, the children learned on their own to imitate her, and they hoarsely panted when she did. Together they sounded like a house of beasts. At first she wondered what it would be like if Matt came home early or if some farmer dropped by, but no one ever came.

She loved the image of herself speeding across the room with the mattock high in the air over her head. "How do you like your old rhinoceros?" she would ask the children sometimes, when she stopped, panting, leaning on the mattock.

When the plastering was down, she chopped out the lathes with an axe. She swung hard so that when the lathing came out, the plaster on the other side, on the dining room wall was chopped through, and fell. This raised so much dust that she made the boys wear bandanas over their noses to strain some of it out, and she worked for a shorter period of time each day.

When the lathes were gone, all that was left of the wall were the upright two-by-six planks. They were spaced eighteen inches apart and stretched from the floor to the ceiling. You could see between the two-by-sixes from one room to the next and get an idea of the airy effect that the place would have when the two rooms were joined. It was like seeing the ribs of a skeleton from the inside. Also, you could now literally walk through the wall. She liked to slip between the two-by-sixes. But eventually she sawed them out. First near the ceiling, then six inches from the floor. They fell over onto the bare floor with a clatter, and she and the children yelled TIMBER for each one.

Debbie regretted that she could not saw them off flush with the floor, but it was too difficult. The six inch stubs were like little teeth embedded recalcitrantly in the floor. Matt paid to have them removed.

She said she wanted the room to be yellow, so they got paint and painted it together. Now that entire side of the house was one large yellow room.

While Matt was gone, Debbie paced around the new space. She wanted to get used to it. In a way she missed the wall. They told themselves that they had greatly increased the value of the property if ever they should want to sell. In fact, maybe they did want to move.

Matt had met a film-maker who was passing through the University. He was young and was looking for people to help him make films. He could use some financial backing, but also just some plain help. Matt gave him a big party and a lot of people from the Philosophy Department and the Poetry Center and the Film Shop drove the forty-five miles down to the farm.

They showed an experimental film that Byron had made and another one that he hadn't made called "Blood of the Beasts." Debbie was pleased that they had the Big Yellow Room for the occasion, but she felt out of touch at the party and kept running upstairs to check on the children. Once she just sat in Matt's study and listened to the noise. She used to enjoy parties in Tennessee. She went down for the films, and suddenly during "Blood of the Beasts" which was about a slaughter house, she found she was furious. It was a terrible film as one animal after another received a blow from a pneumatic hammer, its head was cut off, its hide jerked away. . . . What did that Byron mean bringing such violence into her house!

67

When the guests left, she told Matt how she felt, and Matt was very defensive about the film. He said she just didn't want to face up to where her meat came from. She said *that* wasn't the point, there was something false about the film. He said it was one of the most true films he'd ever seen, and that was the kind of film Byron wanted to make, and Matt wanted to help him. It was a terrible quarrel. They shouted at each other till daybreak. One of the worst things was that the children didn't wake up and cry, but each of them whimpered continually without waking.

The next day at the table Matt said it would do them all good to live in a different sort of place, like New York.

The word touched her like the passing of a wand. Why hadn't he said *New York* last night. She hadn't known that was what the quarrel was about.

He said he hadn't thought that she'd be willing to give up the farmhouse after all the work she'd put into it, but she felt new energy flowing into her.

They weren't able to sell the farmhouse, but they did rent it before they left Iowa. Matt swapped a truck on a Volkswagen bus. They sold their furniture, because Debbie said she wanted to start over. The saddest thing was that Matt couldn't find anybody to take the dogs. The tenant absolutely refused. It wouldn't be fair to the neighbors just to let them run loose, so on the last day, Matt had to take them out in the woods and shoot them. Of course they didn't tell the children, but when Fallow heard the gunshot, he said, "Augggh."

She changed her name to Patience, after her grandmother, which seemed odd to Matt since this was a move to the city, but he had always let Debbie do what she wanted. She wanted to be called Pay for short.

Making films with Byron didn't work out at all. Matt found he could earn money by playing the guitar and singing at birthday parties for rich kids. He understood leisure, and rich people trusted him to be gentle. He enjoyed practicing on his own kids, and they adored him. He had never enjoyed anything so much.

Since he was home anyway much of the time, it meant that Pay didn't have to be there. While the film-making project was going down the drain, Pay met a few more would-be film makers. One of these was a director, and he suggested that since Pay had a background in drama and was so astoundingly good-looking for a mother of three children that she might want to take a small part. She would have to leap over some furniture on stage when a burglar came through the window. She was the housemaid.

"I won't have any trouble with that," she said.

The director was named Thompson and he had a handlebar moustache and wore checked pants. She knew that he was something of a phony, but she liked his energy. Energy was big in New York. In Tennessee it was mostly the women who had to be full of energy and ready for anything, but in New York all the attractive men had that same kind of glitter. Matt really couldn't compete well here, she saw right away. He was just too quiet and lackluster. Oh, he was fine with children; she thought he really had a talent for that, but he couldn't do much with other men.

It made her want to tell him what to do. For his own good, to better himself.

"Are you saying I ought to make more money?" he asked.

In a way, yes, she had to admit it; she was saying make more money. Matt would own ten thousand acres of Tennessee timber when his father died and a share in the Pulaski bank. He didn't see any point in hustling money. He never had. That was one of the things that attracted him about philosophy. It was high-minded, not grubby.

"I don't just sing other people's songs," he said. "I make up my own words and music, too."

Pay could see that the mothers liked Matt a lot. They liked his patience and his gentleness. How he had time to talk with them and make them feel like somebody. It was the way he made her feel during their courtship. Back then all the other guys had seemed so selfish in comparison, and vain, too. Matt so thoroughly forgot that he really wasn't all that good-looking that other women forgot it too. She had forgotten it. He had been so exciting to talk to, back then. Once they had had Thompson over to supper and she watched the way Matt and Thompson had talked. Matt tried to talk to Thompson as though he were a woman, as though he were trying to get him to express how he *felt*.

They went to work on their brownstone—knocked down a wall between the living room and dining room. They even chipped the plaster off the supporting walls to expose the brick. Because they worked together, Pay couldn't run at the walls like a mother rhinoceros. Once when Matt was gone to a birthday party she tried it, but the children had forgotten the game and howled to high heaven. She

70

had left her mattock in Iowa, locked in the windowseat. Matt liked for them to work with large wooden mallets, his a little bit larger than hers.

"There's enough work to keep us both busy here for three years," Pay said.

"I like this work," Matt answered.

"I don't want to do it any more," she said.

Matt said that she really needed to get out of the house more and why didn't she work for the day care center down the street. She thought it was worth a try. Thompson had said sure there was a lot of money to be made in day care in the city.

She read several books on the subject, and she was very impressive to the parents, partly because of her beauty, partly because of her energy. Also she pointed out to the parents that her own beautiful children were there. They remarked how exceptionally bright Fallow was, and she told them how she had saved him. She had the old relationship back with her body, when she told it to move, it moved. She scarcely had to tell it any more. She was pleased that the parents liked her, but she was really in the same position as Matt, she decided—subservient to the real people.

Thompson suggested that they remove a few bricks from the exposed outer wall—it was at least three bricks thick, he claimed—and make a plant niche. After he left, she and Matt had an argument about it. He said it was artsy-fartsy, but as soon as he left for a party, she pried some bricks from the wall. She felt like she was breaking into a safe. The mortar was crumbly and it was very easy to drive a screwdriver into the cracks with the large mallet. She enjoyed every minute of it, and she was delighted to find that Thompson had been telling the truth: there was another layer of bricks behind the one she was removing.

She bought a staghorn fern for the niche and invited Thompson to lunch when Matt was out. Thompson said she ought to see all the plants he had in his place. He had a great place. His bed was up on stilts so he could walk under it and use that space to live in. It was interesting, too, to sleep near the ceiling—a sort of special loft.

She could just imagine it. Suddenly she realized that Thompson was trying to seduce her. She said, "Why *don't* you take me over to see it." The children were already at the day care center. She telephoned to say she'd be two hours late. Thompson was more excited than she was while they walked over to his place. She despised him a little for that, but she was happy, too. She told him how much she wanted to act. Before they climbed the ladder to his bed, he had promised to introduce her to some people in soap opera, to do his best for her.

It wasn't enough.

She began to notice that the father of one of the children at the center was looking at her. He was much more refined than Thompson. He wore expensive clothes and he seemed to care about his little girl, Mary Margaret. He had complete custody of Mary Margaret because her mother was a monster. He had noticed Pay and what a good mother she was, and he wondered if sometimes he could leave MM at her house overnight when he needed to be out of town.

She said she'd have to talk with Matt. It seemed that Matt opposed every project she suggested now. He said that it wasn't genteel to take in kids overnight. Pay said that MM was more like Windy's friend. Matt stalked out of the house, but he soon came back with a potted gardenia for her and said he was sorry, that he wasn't even *thinking* anymore. Pay said they ought to think of ways to be more independent from his father, she reminded him that they hadn't been able to sell the Iowa house. Little Mary Margaret loved to stay with them, and Matt spent more time playing with her than Pay did.

One morning when Royce came for Mary Margaret, Pay took him to see the house. It was kind of an invitation, and he understood. He started bringing Pay little gifts, and usually when he came for Mary Margaret, if Matt was away, he and Pay locked the bedroom door and made love before he went back to his office and took Mary Margaret to day care.

Royce felt guilty about it, said he was breaking up her home-life. He said that it was because she was so beautiful that he just couldn't stop himself from wanting her. Also Royce liked Matt and appreciated his singing, and he said that really made him feel like a rat.

One time all three of them were sitting in the living room with the four children when Matt put down his guitar and started talking philosophically. He said maybe it was wrong for people to stifle their natural impulses toward each other. He went on and on about how possessiveness and jealousy were primitive emotions. Then he said he could see how repression was causing suffering. Pay could see that Royce knew he was talking about them. Royce looked so grateful he could cry. When Matt finished, Royce shook his hand and told him that he'd never met anybody so *noble* before in his life.

After supper Matt and Pay talked more frankly and

decided that they probably needed other people, too.

The next morning Pay knew she despised Matt for what he had said. He'd practically set her free, but she wanted to do it for herself. She decided that she would divorce Matt, and she wouldn't admit anything about Thompson or Royce either.

If she did that, she might lose custody of her children. Whatever else happened, she wanted to keep them. All Matt did was sing, and she couldn't respect that.

She didn't like the kind of work Matt did on the house, and she let herself criticize him whenever she felt like it. They quarreled again and again over the best way to do things. What would increase the value of their property was always the question. Finally they just wanted to get away from each other and there wasn't enough room in the house to do it.

Pay persuaded Matt to move out. Soon afterwards, she ran into him at the deli buying wine with a woman she'd never met.

She called a man she admired from Thompson's play and invited him to spend the night. After that she had many lovers, and she saw Matt with many different women.

Finally, she sued for divorce, asking for the house and, of course, for child support. Also she decided that she didn't want Matt to get to keep the children any, ever. They went to court. Pay knew how to handle the judge. She had known about male judges for a long time.

"Matt made me watch a ghoulish film in my own house with slaughtering in it," she told the judge. "After that he shot our dogs in cold blood."

When it was his turn Matt said that there had been

several weeks between the film and when he shot the dogs.

"But did you shoot them?"

"Yes."

"Didn't you have any feeling for them?"

"That's *why* I shot them. I did love them. You can't leave your dogs to run wild."

Matt had grown a little beard, and as Pay looked at him in court, he looked like a werewolf to her. Instead, she looked up at the judge. She assumed an air of overcoming embarrassment as though she had stumbled on stage and thought as loudly as she could I LOVE YOU. He gave her complete custody of the children.

She went home to the brownstone to be alone before she picked up the children at day care. She sat and looked at the wide blond floor planks that she and Matt had exposed. He had used a high powered sander to get down to the blond wood. Then he had carved tiny wedges, slivers, really, of wood to force into the cracks that had opened over the years as the big boards shrank back from each other. It was too bad that he had to leave the house that he'd worked on so creatively.

She thought that she would try again, now, to get into acting. Now, without Matt, she told herself, she could do whatever she had to in order to win. She asked herself whether she would win—she had won, so far, hadn't she?—but neither her body nor her mind would tell her.

Madame Charpentier and Her Children

"I like his sentence rhythms," I said, speaking of Charles Dickens, to my best friend Amy Carpenter.

"The Nineteenth Century rides again." She looked up at the clouds and said that she liked Robert Coover's inventive form in "The Babysitter."

I swooped into the contemporary after her and criticized a successful woman writer who filled her stories with brand names and condescended to her characters. "She never writes about anybody half as smart as she is," I added.

It was autumn and we had already gone back to teaching, but the grip of the university was still loose and the feeling of summer cradled us. We were sitting on Amy's patio, the prettiest in the city, I thought, at a wrought-iron table painted Chinese red. The sweetgum leaves were topaz. I looked at the sky over her patio and thought *Her sky*, thought of Keats and Shelley but did not mention them, and fell to inspecting Amy's hairdo.

Should I have mine cut to match? Would we talk

about our favorite subject today, in September? I examined her hair, a kind of Dutch bob, square corners in front; mine was what my husband called a Dorothy Hamill cut—rounded, like a bowl had been put on my head. Our long-haired daughters, though hers was ten and mine was four, were playing together amiably on the edge of the woods.

Now we *were* on our favorite subject; one that was too precious, too risky, to discuss often—ourselves, how we were alike and different. It was too precious to talk long about how we were alike; too risky to point out our differences. (Suppose they were truly *significant*, once we aired them?)

"Of course it's better to lie sometimes," she said. "Only a dodo would always tell the truth in intimate circumstances."

I felt the abyss opening between us, my gray cells scrambling. Quickly I invented: "I think it's impossible to tell a lie. A lie only tells something else about you. Probably something even more basic."

Did it matter what we said? I watched the prickly sweetgum balls swing on their stems in the breeze, and the sky was so bright behind them I had to look down. Beast, one of her giant dogs, lay at my feet; a drop of saliva waited at the end of the groove in his long pink tongue. Her cats ambled in and out of the woods. Half a mile on in the woods, a bluff dropped to the Ohio River and across that was Kentucky where Stuart and I lived and taught.

Once Stuart and Stephanie, just a baby then, and I had driven through Concord, during a New England December. Stuart wanted to see the homes of Emerson and Hawthorne; I half-lied and said I did too—I wanted to humor him. All the houses turned out to be closed for the winter. But when we drove past the Alcott house, he made me get out in the snow while he kept the sleeping baby in the car. "Just tramp around. Look in the windows," he said. So I did. When I looked in the low-ceilinged parlor, the flowered wallpaper and flowered carpets clashing mellowly in the afternoon sunlight, I gasped. It was Jo's world. The world that had a girl writer in it. And family love. It was like looking in an Easter egg and seeing my own moment of birth. It was all the more exciting that I could not go in. As I circled the house, I met two other women slogging through the snow, and I saw on both their faces the expression that was surely mine, too.

But sitting on Amy Carpenter's patio, this autumn, being with my friend was like living in a limitless world. It was not excitement, the thrill of peeking in at something permanent, but satisfaction with a moment of slow flux.

I nodded at a scene in a glossy magazine on Amy's table and said, "This picture used to be at the back of my fourth grade classroom."

"Why did you like it?" Amy asked. She picked up a pale, long-haired cat, flipped it on its back and scratched under its chin in a way that made Sunny's eyes close with pleasure. My four-year-old had liked Amy and everything about her so much that she had insisted on giving our cats the same names—Sunny, Furball, Chagall and Pitty Sing.

"I could never decide if I wanted to be the little girl sitting on the sofa next to her mother or the older girl sitting on the dog."

"They're really the same girl," Amy said.

"They're dressed alike."

"That's what I mean," she said, and dumped Sunny onto the patio.

Amy's lover, Maxey, came through the French doors, with her husband Alexander, who was mad, right behind him.

"You'll have to call the repair man," her lover said.

"There's water all over the kitchen floor now," her husband said, trying to substitute irony for anger in his voice. Alex was a tall, gaunt, raptorial man, a lawyer. He was handsome in a fierce way; he had a large, hooked mustache shaped like the horns of a water buffalo.

"If I just had the right part, those valves—" Maxey began.

"Well, clean it up," Amy said cheerfully to her husband, but to her lover she said, "Maxey, you don't have to fix the dishwasher. Sit out here and talk to Harriet and me."

Maxey selected a chocolate-filled croissant from the silver tray and sat with us. Alexander muttered that he'd be out in a bit; he snapped a damp dishcloth at the air and went back to the kitchen. Maxey bit the tip off the croissant and looked miserable.

"Cheer up," Amy said sympathetically. "Alexander wouldn't have tried to fix it by himself."

"Do you like this painting?" I asked him.

Maxey shrugged and looked up at the sky. "You need a new swivel on that windsock," he said. "It must have rusted out. It won't face into the wind like it should."

"Don't lay a hand on that sucker," Alex shouted from the kitchen.

Maxey looked morose. I silently urged him to jolly up. I knew Amy had no patience with self-inflicted gloom. It was one of the ways she was a tonic for me. With her, I didn't dare display the self-pity I was prone to indulge in, and when I didn't show it, the sadness went away. Better than that, being with Amy replaced remorse with something giddy.

Amy shoved *Smithsonian* under Maxey's defeated nose and repeated my question, "Do you like this picture?"

Maxey sighed, "Not particularly. Too sweet. Renoir's always sentimental."

"No, he's not," Amy said. "Look at that face."

Amy was interested in Madame Charpentier, not the girls. I had always avoided Madame Charpentier's face because it was disappointingly nonexpressive. It was the daughters, so much alike, but surely different by virtue of their places in the painting, whose world I wanted to enter.

"See," she went on, "Renoir knows Madame Charpentier's bored to death. She's just sitting to please her husband. Her husband wants to picture her like that, an art object, just with her children. Maternal. She wants to be holding her *salon*, talking to somebody interesting."

I went on for her, "Renoir knows that the husband will never look once at his wife's face in the painting. He'll look at the picture for years and never register that part." I had repressed my own response to that placid face for years.

"Well, why do you like it then?" Maxey asked me. He was no slouch; he knew I'd shifted myself onto Amy's turf: I hadn't had the slightest interest in the adult figure.

I told Maxey that I liked the dog, the large black and white spaniel, how its patterning was like Madame Charpentier's dress. Things seemed so fast-paced and bright when I was with Amy and Maxey. Years ago in the fourth grade, I loved to sit in the desk just in front of a copy of the Renoir picture. While I read, I leaned my shoulder inside the frame. Sometimes I sneaked a glance behind the picture to see the twisted wire and the brown paper that

81

backed their world. "I was always surprised," I was able to tell Stuart, later.

To Maxey I repeated only how the two little girls, so pretty in their blue and white party dresses, their fragile hair, had fascinated me, though I could see Maxey was getting bored.

"Maxey, rub my neck, please," Amy said.

I felt uncomfortable watching his small, practiced hands move over her neck and shoulders, but Amy always did just what she wanted.

Stuart, my husband, came up to the patio from the woods with a baby rabbit cupped in his hands. Both our daughters ran to see it, and Amy's husband, the dishcloth trailing from his back pocket, came out of the kitchen.

They made a pretty group: the two men and the two little girls who looked like them. It was in their firm chins and their definite little jaws that both the daughters looked like their fathers—as though they'd all been painted by an artist who could only show family resemblance in that one feature. The girls were still in shorts and tee shirts, but Amy and I had acknowledged the fall in their colors, gold for her Peggy and plum for my Stephanie. Their fathers were both dressed in beige and white, pale and sculptural. The group was composed by Stuart's hands in the center and the rabbit.

"Peggy wants to cut her hair," Amy said.

"Oh, tell her not to. It's beautiful long."

When I was in college, my best friend and I had been pictured together in the yearbook with the snide caption *Wonder who their hair stylist is?* We both had long dark hair past our shoulders, and it was decidedly unkempt. Not that Molly or I cared.

82

"Bring it over here, Stuart," Amy called.

Stuart looked up at her and grinned, even his eyes smiling, as though he were looking at a fond thing in looking at my friend Amy Carpenter.

Eyes are not Stuart's best feature. I suppose they are mine. Amy says I have smart eyes. My boyfriend in college, who got killed, had truly smart eyes.

The friendship between Amy and me remained the same, through the year. I loved driving across town and across the river to Amy's house. Driving to the home of a friend is a wonderful pleasure to me—better than the anticipation of opening a present you hold in your lap. The present may disappoint; the friendship only becomes more complex and interesting. I was an adult and in college before I became conscious of the going-to-visit pleasure, but then it swept over me often when I drove to Married Barracks to visit my friend Molly Stevens. Once while I drove I thought of a metaphor for Molly and me: our minds were like two meadows, lying side by side, with no fence, and sometimes it was hard to tell where one meadow ended and the other began—just so freely, we crossed back and forth mentally.

Perhaps the pleasure of driving to Molly Stevens's barracks had been even greater than this present pleasure, for I had been close to her husband, too. With Alexander, I always felt that we shared some inarticulate secret which made me clumsy with him. Actually, Stuart and I thought of Amy's and Alexander's place as Amy's Estate. It was out in the country, the house was big and the grounds were big. Stuart and I and Amy were all college teachers and could never have afforded such a setup, but Alexander was a corporate lawyer and bought Amy all that she asked for. Everything that Amy owned was fun to look at—marble eggs, pewter platters, hunting horns, wreaths with ribbons and dried herbs, cherry furniture, Hadley pottery, rugs from India. I always love the possessions of my friends—even the cut of their hair—though never my own. Molly had had a driftwood lamp with a pebble base; to me the crazy lamp was a work of art, and the yellow light it shed was like love.

Molly was poor, of course, and sometimes borrowed money from me, but Amy had a private decorator and a housekeeper. What I loved was the order there, and the quality of the order. The inside of the house was constantly redecorated, walls changing colors faster than the seasons, but it seemed to be a world as stable as a painting. Molly Stevens had spent the money on travel; at her barracks she had been messier than I was.

The little house Stuart and I owned was chaotic—newspapers, magazines, Stuart's sculpture tools, my drafts of plays, our business papers everywhere. From outside, our house did have some cottage charm, dormer windows upstairs, the white paint peeling off enough to show the rosy bricks, bay windows downstairs. It was when they were at our house, the next summer, that I knew things had changed and were going to change.

By *they*, I mean Amy and her lover Maxey. When Amy visited us, it was always with Maxey, who was a college teacher like us and understood flexible schedules, household mess and rapport.

The change in our friendship, mine and Amy's, was nothing dramatic. It was nothing I could put in a play because it was a sort of Henry James occurrence. Suddenly

84

the light falls differently across a face, or you happen to be looking when two people exchange a glance that they believe you don't see. When Henry James tried to write plays, he was a flop. His fiction looks good on TV though, like *The Golden Bowl*, because the camera and screen can be intimate enough to register just those quick lights and angles.

What did I see? What do I see now when I recall the change in my friendship with Amy Carpenter? There is a teapot at the center of it; the teapot is gleaming white decorated with dark blue arabesques. I am sitting on a red camelback sofa in my living room and a south window is to my back; my little daughter Stephanie is sitting beside me. She has a scraped knee. It is my birthday, in midsummer, and they are all leaving me, but first presents from Amy and Maxey, and champagne served by Stuart in V-shaped glasses. We allow Stephanie to dip her finger in my crystal glass and to suck champagne from her finger or dabble her hurt knee with it. Yellow ribbons from the opened present, the white and blue teapot, fall across my lap and Stephanie's. The room is full of sunlight. Amy says to me, *Your house has more light in it than mine*, and I can hear the disbelief in her voice because her house cost four times as much as mine. I want to tell her how I have been very careful about buying the light, how I refused all houses without it.

"Thank you," I say, for the teapot.

"I love this teapot," Amy says, "I have one just like it."

And then she glances at Stuart, and I know, quick as that, why, she's been kissing Stuart. And the light changes. It actually does, as though I have grown faint, and I am looking in a dark place, peeking in some car at night, like looking in a dark egg, and there they are, kissing.

"Look," Stephanie says, "it makes rainbows," and she holds up Maxey's little gift, inexpensive and perfect as always, a prism, threaded with a clear monofilament.

"Thank you," I say desperately, and we all drink more champagne and now they are about to leave, to go on one of those eternal retreats, an academic conference on how to retain the freshman student, and I will be alone for five days, starting with my fortieth birthday, with Stephanie. And my husband and my two best friends are getting up and making exit conversation—"How'd you hurt your knee," Maxey asks Stephanie.

"Climbing a tree."

"Now who told you to climb a tree?" he teases.

"The tree."

"Which one of those limbs said, 'Come climb me?'" (She's four, don't push her so hard, I want to say.)

"The *whole* tree said so," she answers.

I feel a rush of pride in her.

"Did your bad feet make you do it? What part told you?"

"My heart."

Maxey shuts up, and I feel fierce tears in my eyes, in my joy that she can protect herself.

"Well, let's go," Amy says. She has her own room at the conference, but she and Maxey will spend every night together.

"Got your things packed?" Maxey says to Stuart in a patronizing way, and, as we stand up, I know how they have decided that Stuart is suffering too much in monogamy, how they will encourage him to have an affair at the conference, with anyone—they don't care who—and how they will promise to keep his secret.

After they go, after I close the front door, I turn and there is the southern light pouring into the room, the window beyond the sofa so ablaze that the green world is gone in its dazzling.

Some things I know. There is such a sudden connection between my eyes and my heart that the truth is undeniable. No amount of hoping, wishing, even plotting can change it. How do I know that I know? What's to say these intuitions are not paranoia? A good scientific question. One that appeals to my smart side, the rational part. But when I have had this sudden knowledge, later experience verifies it. Always.

Once, when I was a college student, I drove past a bus stop and saw the most beautiful young woman I had ever seen. She had a perfect face and one long brown braid hanging down her back. I knew that my boyfriend, the young man who was later killed in an auto accident, would fall in love with her if he ever saw her. He and I were so much alike, our aesthetic so in tune, that he could not escape falling in love with her. My only hope was that he might never see her. But the campus was small, he did see her, and he did fall in love with her. Oh, we remained dear friends, he and I. And now he is dead. He could have loved her forever, married her and lived happily ever after, if it had been up to me, if it would have kept him alive.

"Alive, alive, O!"—Molly used to sing from an Irish folk song. Her death was by her own hand, no accident. Aimed at me, at her husband, at all of us who could not, or would not, satisfy her. I thought of Alex, who would spend anything to please Amy, and I thought of myself, who said no. No more money; I can't give it to you and go to graduate school.

When they came back from the freshman retention conference, I tried not to see Amy often. What could I say? I know by the tone of your voice, I know by the light in your eyes that you have not been my true friend. No, I would hold steady, give no sign of what I knew, but I would try not to look at her. I would hold steady for Stuart, too, praise the erotic torsos that he loved to chisel, the headless women. I would keep Stephanie's world intact. Just as Amy saved her patio, her high windsock, her gold-encrusted china, the seasons of her rooms—all for her daughter.

I would do anything for you Molly had said to me, finally. *You rub my back. Why don't you want the rest of me? Why won't you really love me?*

I had the phone taken out in my new tiny room at my new university so that I wouldn't have to hear her, so that I wouldn't ride waves of panic, as I listened to her expensive, long-distance voice, at the cost of it all. Molly's husband, in the end, had to telegraph me at my new graduate school *The world is split in two.*

Early in the fall, Amy came to my front door, unexpectedly, dramatically. I saw her face crumble just before she threw herself into my arms, my arms ready to catch her, automatically, my face ready to cry, whatever her sorrow.

"I told Maxey it was over," she said.

I knew where we were. They had been lovers for eight years, but from time to time, they tried to get away from each other.

"Oh, you'll make up," I said. I said it as kindly as I

could, still stiff internally, though I held her comfortingly.

"No," she sobbed. "This is it."

Usually she didn't cry. I knew she need not cry now. I knew it was a drama to enlist my sympathy, but I was touched. It is not easy to perform a passion. Suppose you can't carry it off? Suppose you are seduced by the role into a desperate new corner of your psyche? She cared for me; she was willing to risk all this, to keep me.

"What did he say?" I asked. "Did you break it off, or Maxey?"

"I did," she said. "And he said 'Good!' "

"Now come inside and have some tea," I said. "Stuart and Stephanie are at the zoo."

I got out my birthday teapot, and we sat at the kitchen table among some newspapers spotted with clay.

"Do you like the pot?" Amy said between sniffles.

"Yes," I said. "It was a perfect present."

This much I never did know: how much did she know I knew? As this second fall passed into winter I sometimes felt that I had been a coward, a child, that I should have aired with Amy my suspicion. But it was not suspicion. It was knowledge. Gained from the air, gained from the light, without evidence, but knowledge. Aesthetic knowledge, I guess. What would be gained by making us both uncomfortable? This was exactly the same reason that Amy would have decided not to tell me, if she knew my husband was unfaithful. So we were just alike in our impulses after all, and why drive us apart with what would take the voice of accusation?

One rainy dark night just before Christmas, we four—Maxey and Amy, and Stuart and I—took a visiting speaker to a bar. We were glad to be in charge of him; by semester's end academia has become dry and much needs watering by these social occasions. Besides, Amy and I had both loved the speaker, simply because he was so smart. We had glanced at each other in the auditorium and known how the other loved this mind that seemed more congenial than that which either Maxey or Stuart could offer.

In the bar, Amy and I sat on either side of him, not to compete, but to cooperate, to discover in the brief time that we had with him before he left that which both of us would most enjoy knowing. It was sexual. We knew his mind, knew his beautiful nose so straight and perfect as to break your heart, but how was he, as a lover of women?

Usually, I hate bars—too dark and too noisy to see and hear the way you have to, to get the interesting stuff. But this time, I was lucky. The candle was right in front of Dwight McFee; he cradled it with his hands, warming them compulsively, and Amy and I leaned forward so that we could see each other full face, beyond his profile and downcast eyes.

Purposefully Amy let her eyes seem to follow some guy across the room. "He looks just like my first lover," Amy said.

"How old were you?" I asked.

"Seventeen," she said.

Dwight McFee glanced at her, surprised at her frankness.

"I was twenty-five," I said. He looked at me.

"Was it good?" she asked.

At the next table, Stuart and Maxey had started debating something our speaker had said, in passing, about artificial intelligence.

"It was wonderful," I said, and meant it. Dwight looked at me again.

"I was jammed into a car seat," Amy said. "Outside my dorm. When I went in I thought everybody knew. I thought they could tell by looking at my eyes."

Dwight laughed.

I said, "I used to sleep at home with a string tied around my big toe. The string hung out the window with my name on it. I thought if my boyfriend was prowling around the back yard, he might pull it, and then we'd have sex."

"Really?" Amy said. In the candlelight, her eyes were sparkling with disbelief, that anyone could be so naive. I'd never told her this before, and she thought I might be making it up. But I never make things up.

Dwight believed me.

"Did he pull the string?" Dwight asked.

"No," I said. I wouldn't tell him my friend got killed. I just said *No*. But because Dwight could feel the heavy sadness that was real in me, then he told us about his first time.

"She was a neighbor, beautiful young woman, pregnant, about twenty. I was eleven years old . . ." he began.

It was the bizarre and wonderful event that Amy and I not just wanted to know but *needed* to know, to have him.

"How pregnant?" Amy wanted to know. I felt I knew.

"At term," he said. He looked at her steadily and refused to elaborate.

"Yes," I said. "Round as a pumpkin. Round as a coach."

On the drive home, through wet arches of Christmas

91

lights, Stuart said to me, "You know how borzoi hunt wolves? They hunt in pairs." He put his arm around me. "Two of them run together, they're extremely fast, and one gets on one side of the wolf and one gets on the other. Then they grab the wolf at the same time on either side of the jaws. They don't injure the wolf, they just hold it till the hunter comes."

I was much taken with the story.

"You and Amy," he said. "You're just like a pair of borzoi."

We were. I was full of satisfaction. And then, looking at the reflections of the colored lights in the wet street, I knew something else: Stuart and Amy weren't kissing anymore.

The next time I visited Amy at her house—it was only a few days later, almost Christmas—was the best time. It was her best present, my Christmas present really.

Amy phoned to ask Stuart to drop Stephanie over early, so I was gloriously alone for the drive. As I crossed the bridge, I knew that I would feel especially comfortable at Amy's, right from the start. Stuart and Alexander would be hiking out in the woods for at least another hour. I was so happy that I sang while I drove. Molly had had a beautiful singing voice; Amy could barely play the giant black Steinway in her library. I felt secure in their differences: Molly was full of warmth though she wanted to be given everything, finally my body and my soul. Amy was prickly with wit, but her hands were open, for me.

I parked in the *porte cochère*, and let myself in the back door. Amy called from the living room in a voice that was almost singing, musical and inviting.

"Come on in. We're in here, Harriet."

I stood at the doorframe of the living room and looked in. Nineteenth century, she was wearing a black *salon* dress with a dazzling jabot, a froth of lace at the neck. Nestled next to her, my Stephanie, with her frock so blue and white as to risk sentimentality, gazed out at me. One of the dogs, brown and white instead of the black and white spaniel, lay beside the sofa, and Peggy, dressed in the same pastoral hues of blue and cloud, sat on the dog's coarse hip. Amy's dress was a night of blackness, a hundred planes of witty sophistication, the jabot more precise than I remembered in its stiff laciness, in its realism. Was there something erotic in her pose? Something quite other than Madame Charpentier's maternal composure? I gasped and looked in her eyes. Not bored. Not mocking. Inviting me to come in, to be that person, or like her.

Carefully, I leaned my shoulder inside the flared frame of the door, hesitated, and then crossed the air to move into those colors, that glowing.

Five Lessons
from a Master Class

Both Mother and Joel are pianists. Whose playing I prefer depends on which one I heard initially on a particular piece. Soon after I met Joel, he played the Ravel *Pavane for a Dead Princess* for me—I loved the dry way he played the left hand against the lyric *legato* of the right hand—and, after that, I never liked to hear Mother play it at all. But I had heard her Chopin all my life, and, for me, Joel couldn't touch her there. His Bach was better—he played the organ as well as the piano—but her Beethoven suited me. They were never jealous of each other. The three of us lived together and he was endlessly courteous to her. On the other hand, I always thought she had some slight reservation about him—though she adored him.

At age seventy-eight, my mother could pass for sixty. I suppose years of using Pond's cold creme had kept her complexion relatively youthful. Her arthritis had not affected her hands at all. She played the piano as well as ever—though perhaps a little less accurately.

When we were courting, Joel told me that as much as he cared for me he really admired my mother more. I didn't mind, but I was curious. "She plays well, doesn't she?" I said.

"She plays with integrity," he answered.

Once I tried playing for Joel—a Brahms *Intermezzo*. He swooped down on me and said, "Here, let me do that," and then he played it very well, personally for me—exactly as I had heard it in my mind. I felt cherished in a way that I had never thought possible.

Joel was enormously talented, but he did not care to be a professional musician. Maybe my mother distrusted that decision. He had a series of jobs in counselling. The agencies Joel worked for were always running out of funds, and it was necessary for him to get some sort of new job, from time to time. But he was wonderful with young people.

Joel had slightly extravagant tastes—not selfish tastes, but he would spend money—one time on a painting he admired, another time on an oriental carpet aflutter with birds. When he had the blue patio slate delivered, Mother watched out the kitchen window, frowned as the workmen unloaded the stones, and said, "I'll bet that cost a pretty penny."

But Joel put the stones in himself so that he would be satisfied with the aesthetic effect.

Four weeks later when Mother and I were sitting on the patio under the elm, she suddenly remarked, "I believe this is the most beautiful patio I have ever seen."

I agreed with her: the patio was stunning in the most understated and restful of ways. Joel had flanked it on one side with rhododendrons and ferns; on the sunny edge, he had daffodils, peonies and day lilies. He planted tulips in the shade—that was the master stroke. They were a brilliant scarlet, but in the shadows. Of course they wouldn't come back the next year. He would pull them as soon as they bloomed and put in tuberous begonias, already in bloom from the nursery. In the fall, he would replant with new tulip bulbs. He told me that when you got tulips to come back the next year, the blooms were always smaller and less satisfactory.

I guess Mother knew I was worried about the money. I taught senior high school English—hard work and low pay. But I did have a miraculously good situation, at a public high school within walking distance of our house. The principal was an elderly woman who had made the place her garden for thirty years. She had the figure of a cumulus cloud—all billows, bulges, softness—and she wore nylon jersey dresses printed all over with flowers. Mrs. Tibbs gave a talk to every freshman class and somehow managed to make nearly all the students want to work. I admired her enormously, even loved her.

But the pay was poor, and I started tutoring college students who were failing freshman English. Joel was always taking on extra jobs, too. He was great at directing musicals, but sometimes he did it just for fun, so it didn't really add that much to the family coffers. My mother had her Social Security money, and she chipped in some of it. We had to grub, though we lived in a home with a landscaped yard.

I once asked Mrs. Tibbs if she couldn't do something about the fact that her wonderful staff was woefully underpaid. "Dedication is what this business is all about," she said. "And that means low pay." I wondered whether the size of Elmer Tibbs's salary had underwritten Mrs. Tibbs's attitude, but when I inquired of an older teacher, I learned that Mr. Tibbs was an invalid and hadn't turned a dime in thirty years.

Mrs. Tibbs was a good deal like my mother. I was surprised that Joel didn't like her. "She's a dragon, isn't she?" he said. I told him that I got along with her very well. "You would," he said sweetly.

Just before summer vacation—that is the great humane thing about teaching, that three months—Mother pointed out an announcement in *Clavier* magazine about a master piano class out in Oklahoma, in early June. The teacher was a woman with a long and highly successful career as a concert artist.

"Probably it wouldn't be so terribly hot, then," Mother said. "It's not expensive either."

We sent off for their literature, which turned out to include a photograph of the latest class. The teacher, with massive gray hair piled up high on her head, was grinning broadly at the camera. Another woman, young enough to be Madame's daughter but identified as her assistant, had her hair piled up in the same way. One woman in the class appeared to be older than Mother.

Mother suggested that she go as an auditor, rather than as a performer. I tried weakly to persuade her to sign up to play for Madame, but something told me that she was probably right to want to audit. Of course there was no decision to be made about my own status; my ability was about that of a musical, but limited, twelve-year-old.

It made no difference that music and literature were different disciplines—I would examine everything Madame said, even her body language, to take back to my students. Best, the music would be unending—like inheriting a stranger's perennial garden of continuous and surprising bloom. Still, I wouldn't have made the drive or the investment of time except that I knew it would make Mother supremely happy.

Joel teased me a little about my thinking that the session possibly would improve my playing, but he really did want us to go and have a good time. It meant for two weeks he would have to take the bus to get to the Youth Guidance Center.

It took us five days to get from Cincinnati to Tulsa; the trip was quite hard on both of us. On the second day Mother's ankles began to swell, so I had her sit in the back seat with her feet up. Every two hours I stopped so that we could exercise. I didn't want her to feel lonesome, or like a burden back there, so I was always twisting my head back to say something. I knew she didn't catch a lot of it—she is quite hard of hearing—but she always appeared alert and comfortable enough when I looked back. Looking back kept me dizzy and disoriented much of the time.

We stayed at cheap motels without attached restaurants, and we ate fast food along the way. Mother had never eaten fast food, and she was quite cheerful about it.

Our first night out, when we called home, Joel said that he had played organ for the spontaneous wedding of one of our friends. I hadn't even known Guy had been thinking about getting married. Joel asked if I remembered Samantha Snow from high school—a friend of the bride who had known me. I remembered Samantha as having a beautiful singing voice, though untrained. Joel said she was working at a garden shop now, had never married.

Later when I asked Mother whether she remembered Samantha, Mother said, "She was a knockout back then, wasn't she?" When I told her about the wedding, she said,

"One of those so-called impromptu things where all the friends do things for free, huh?"

I decided not to tell her that Joel had played for nothing, and that Samantha had donated flowers. Or that Joel said he had invited her out to see our back yard.

Sometimes I felt so anxious about the weather that I thought I would burst into tears while I was driving. As we went west, it got hotter and hotter. The car was not air-conditioned, and I knew how heat exhausted Mother. We bought a little styrofoam cooler in St. Louis and loaded it with fruit juices. Neither she nor I expressed any anxiety about anything. But all along the way, after the telephone call and when Mother was asleep, I worried about the weather.

One: The Lesson of Joy

"When Madame arrives," her assistant said, "We will all rise and applaud. These courtesies mean a great deal to Madame."

We were seated on bleachers on the stage of the university recital hall. I was delighted to see that the student who had looked even older than Mother was among the students again.

Madame entered grandly wearing trousers that were close-fitting at the ankles, and a tunic. She looked casual and comfortable, though her hair was piled high, concert-style, and she wore high-heeled sandals. Her ankles were as trim as mine. She was seventy-two years old, but she bristled with energy. Really, it was shocking. She seemed *frisky*. I saw at once that her marvelous body, her endurance and her whole nervous system were a part of her genius.

She stood between the twin grand pianos and bowed to us, thanking us for the applause. She flashed the expansive grin of the photograph and said rather formally, "May I welcome you." Then her face closed as quickly as a drawstring purse, and she was all business, introducing the first performer, who was from Alberta, Canada. Obviously, there was nothing to talk about, nothing high-flown or theoretical about the art of music, until there was music.

The Canadian played from the Chopin *Etudes, Op. 25*. The music was a bath of loveliness for me, but I forced myself to write my opinion as well: *wonderful rippling sound, too much bass though, top line maybe a little disconnected, a bit dabby. Could use a little more dynamic shading, but the basic shape is present.*

Madame's response began with formal courtesy: "Very nice, very, very nice." Then her face concentrated itself again, and she said, "This is too slow for its character. The tempo is the piece. And the accompaniment is too loud in the bass, too." Ah, something I had noted.

She familiarly picked up the young man's wrist. "The wrist must be more flexible. The thumb is not free." She leaned over the keyboard, and from her standing position played a single chord with her left hand. I couldn't believe it. The playing of the single chord had an authority, had a coherence that was far beyond any sound produced by the highly gifted student. "See, give it a more open sound. The wrist is up. A steep angle to the thumb. Which finger must be fixed as an axis? The third finger—don't lose it as an anchor point."

She stood up to look into the student's eyes. He was so cowed, he could only nod. She went on, "Now the right

101

hand. The third finger is still the anchor point. The top note is like picking a harp. The left hand must be softer. It has no shine to it—the fifth is not there."

She seemed to decide that he had taken all the criticism he could absorb. "But you have a very nice sound. . . ." Yet, she was not quite ready for closure, "But it's not quite safe. The fingers don't quite do the job. They're too weak. You spread them. Get in real contact with the key." Now she was finished.

I saw that courteousness and tact were for the sake of the human performer. The technical comments were for the music, which was what she really cared about. That was not true for me; I did care about my students. But then, she had never seen the Canadian before, anyway.

When the next performer, a young Korean woman, finished her movement of a Beethoven sonata, Madame exclaimed with more enthusiasm, "Very good. Excellent." With just the alertness of her face, this performer conveyed that she really wanted to hear all Madame might say; she wasn't going to waste her opportunity to learn by being cowed. The feedback was a barrage of information about the deportment of particular fingers at particular moments in the piece. As soon as Madame got the words out of her mouth, the student instantly followed the verbal direction. "Have the second finger in the air; let go of the bottom fast," Madame said, and it was instantly done. "Superb!"

At the end, Madame entered only one non-technical comment. She picked up the woman's hand and held it tenderly, almost. "You have a small hand," she said. She quickly let go of it and held her own hand up for us all to see: "But this is the most small hand that exists."

Thus— I noted—*she snatches back the spotlight from*

her student for herself.

I felt sorry for the next student—he looked miserably frightened, though his jaw was set as though he felt it disgraceful—unmanly even—to allow himself to be afraid of Madame. After he played the first movement of the Mozart *Concerto in B Flat, K. 45*, she said with perceptible impatience, "May I first praise you to high heaven—don't look so grim." She turned to the class, "Now what's wrong with this concerto?" She glared at the group.

"God gave him such a talent," she went on, obviously speaking of Mozart, "that every experience transforms itself into music. Arrive joyfully at the high point." She broke off to say to the student, "The listener doesn't know that you've started."

"What was missing," she went on, "was *joy*. This is a ravishing work. You must note by note embody joy!"

At this moment my mother leaned over and wrote in my notebook: *I will bring my cushion next time!*

I realized she couldn't understand very much of what was said.

"The left hand must never budge, but the right hand is free. Your hand is excellent, but you don't use it. Chromatics are always charged, loaded in this music." She stopped to peer at him, with no hint of a smile. "I understand you want to work with me next semester."

"Yes."

"I'll kill you in the process."

When we were in our dormitory room, I lay on top of the sheet and listened to my mother snore. I listened, too, to the aged air conditioner engage and disengage. The room was almost cool enough. I worried about the heat.

103

Would we be all right in there if the temperature rose five degrees?

Before bedtime, I had talked with Joel on the telephone and learned that Samantha had loved our yard. They'd had lemonade on the patio, then planted a basket of pansies together. Joel had played his own accompaniment and sung "Der Lindenbaum" for her. Then Joel had played, and she had sung some Schubert songs. I had asked if she were any good.

Excellent, Joel had said.

As I lay on the top sheet, I heard his voice again— *excellent*—and recognized the timbre of joy.

Two: The Lesson of Kindness

When we stepped out of the dormitory the next morning, we flinched from the light and heat.

"The light needs some getting used to," Mother said.

"Yes," I answered and got a pair of sunglasses out of my purse for each of us. We didn't mention the heat, since there was nothing we could do about it. I felt moisture gathering between my shoulder blades; Mother's forehead looked dewy. The sidewalk ahead of us was blazing.

As we seated ourselves in the bleachers, I was surprised to see several children among the class. I noticed a tiny, dark Indian girl sitting beside her mother, who was dressed in a sari and had a red caste mark on her forehead.

"Now," Madame said, "we have little Laura." She held out her hand, and the Indian girl approached timidly. "Sit down, little Laura."

Laura played a short minuet from the Magdalena

Bach Notebook. She made many mistakes, and the tempo was uneven. She seemed unaware that she was playing poorly. I watched her mother, but her face was without expression. I could have played as well.

"Thank you, dear," Madame said. "Kay," she spoke sharply to her assistant, "was I sent the tape for little Laura?"

Kay answered with a single syllable in the affirmative.

"No," Madame went on. "It is not possible."

I was sure Madame was right. Certainly the child did not need to be instructed by one of the world's greatest pianists. Any teacher with patience could have helped her— a little.

"But you are here in any case, aren't you?" Madame said to Laura. "And how old are you, Laura?"

Laura stared at Madame and said nothing.

Madame sighed. She turned to us, sitting in the bleachers. "And is Laura's teacher here?"

For a moment no one moved. The Indian woman leaned over and said something into the ear of the old lady whose picture mother and I had noticed in the class photo from the previous year. Slowly, the old lady stood up.

"Laura comes from El Paso," she said. Her voice shook, not at all from fear but simply with the palsy of old age.

"And you are her teacher," Madame said. She held herself stiffly. I realized that they were both old ladies— surely no more than ten years difference in their ages, but one was worn, soft as an old rag, and the other was like iron lace.

"You would be amazed," the old lady said, "at the *words* she knows."

"But that is not our business, is it?" Madame said.

"We teach Laura music. How long has she been studying with you?"

Suddenly the Indian woman was standing beside the old lady. She bowed to Madame and then said, "We are so grateful to Mrs. Martin for teaching Laura."

My mother leaned over and wrote in my notebook: *What are they saying?*

I wrote back: *They're talking about her background.*

Mother wrote: *What eyes! Such a little deer!*

Madame shrugged, "What can I say? Is it possible for her to have another teacher?"

The old lady turned toward the Indian woman; she had not understood the question.

"Laura has had no teacher but Mrs. Martin. Mrs. Martin has taught her everything. She has learned all the beautiful music from Mrs. Martin. She is our neighbor."

"Thank you," Madame said. She turned from them, but they remained standing. Madame approached Laura who had stared at the keyboard while the adults talked. "Now, Laura, play it for me again. Maybe a little more slowly. You must not get in the habit of playing this piece too slowly, but for now, we will try it that way, all right? Try to keep your hands together."

Laura played again, as miserably as before. When she finished, her old teacher feebly clapped her hands.

"Please!" Madame said, "This is my class." She glared at Mrs. Martin. "Thank you, little Laura. That is all. When you practice, try to keep your hands together. Whatever tempo you establish in the beginning—fast or slow—try to play the entire piece at that tempo. Not partly fast, partly slow when the more difficult parts come, you see."

Laura quickly got up and stood between her mother

and her teacher. Each of them took one of her hands, and her mother bent to whisper in her ear.

"Kay," Madame said, "give the mother a list of some teachers close to El Paso."

"She was incredibly cruel," I said to Joel on the phone. "I'm glad mother couldn't hear what she said."

"I think she was afraid."

"Mother?" The idea made me afraid.

"Madame. What she saw in the old lady was infirmity. What she might well come to—who knows when. In ten years, tomorrow, if she had a stroke."

If it happened on stage, Mother would rescue her. My mother would be the one who would remain calm, who would send Kay to call an ambulance, who would turn down the collar of Madame's tunic, who would feel Madame's neck for the pulse.

"That's a kind explanation," I said to Joel, but I wondered if it were true. I missed him. I wanted to make love.

"Samantha says we ought to have some baskets of jasmine and some lilies—not day lilies—lilium."

"I don't like to stake things," I said quickly.

"We can get short ones that don't need staking. She's bringing a catalog tomorrow."

"How kind," I said and could feel bewilderment in my voice. "I remember her as being like a lily."

"Yes. Her hair is long and pale."

I didn't know what to say.

"She's a quick learner," Joel went on. "I gave her some pointers on phrasing."

After the phone call, I went down to the TV room.

107

Terrel, another of the auditors, was there. He was an odd-looking man with a big head and yet a narrow face. The combination made his eyes curve around, like a swimmer's goggles. He was watching a horror film; he said it was one in a series. I liked the kind of voice he had—gentle and firm.

On color TV—we had an inexpensive black and white set at home since Joel didn't like TV—the blood was shocking. I let my hand stray against Terrel's. When he put his arm across my shoulders, I said *No* in a cruel tone.

After I went back to my room, I lay awake and thought how disappointed Mother would be if something went wrong with my second marriage. She hadn't cared much for Robert—literally the boy next door and without a musical bone in his body. I suppose I had married him as an act of rebellion. I thought of all the other people who cared about me, like Mrs. Tibbs, and who would feel bad if Joel and I couldn't stay together.

Once Mrs. Tibbs came to my Senior English class and read King Lear's storm speech—"Strike flat the thick rotundity of the world." I had been surprised and thrilled by Mrs. Tibbs's performance, but when she said at the end, "I should have been Sir Laurence Olivier," a squirt of unkind laughter escaped from me.

Later, when I heard Olivier do the speech, I was astonished to find myself thinking that Mrs. Tibbs really had done it better.

Three: The Lesson of Death

When Mother and I awoke the next morning, we both noticed that our room was already warm, despite the

108

air conditioning. We didn't say anything about it, but we both put on culottes and wore white sleeveless blouses. As soon as we stepped out of the building, the heat enveloped us. We plunged ahead, through the shade and up the glaring sidewalk. Before we were halfway up the walk, a triangle of perspiration stuck the fabric to her back.

Then something nice happened. Terrel came hurrying to join us, and he chatted in such an interesting and pleasant way that we forgot to notice the heat. Terrel told us about Madame's incarceration in a Japanese prison camp during World War II. She had been in Japan on a concert tour and had been imprisoned on some sort of spying charge. Her status as an artist had been disregarded and she was set to scrubbing floors. Eventually someone did realize that she was a great pianist and allowed her to play an old upright piano for two hours on Sunday afternoons.

When we stood for her entrance on the stage, I admired her body again. She would have scrubbed the floor with endless energy. If that was what her body had to do for her, it would have done it. She was a person who *was* her nervous system, and hers was oceanic in its energy.

As a young Latin woman with shoulder-length black hair seated herself at the piano, Mother reviewed her schedule and wrote in my notebook: *Schubert is M's specialty, you know.*

Terrel leaned down from the bleacher just above us and whispered, "This will be a treat."

He was right. I had never heard the Schubert *Opus Posthumous in B-Flat Major* before, but the opening melody moved me a great deal. I made no attempt to critique the performance in my notebook. After the title of the piece, I simply wrote: *lovely. Ask Joel to learn,* and drew a star.

At the end, Madame quietly said, "Yes. Yes. That is very nice. . . . But"—here she glanced up at the young woman as though to judge whether she were capable of understanding what was about to be said—"but this is something different. We will work only on the opening phrase. Play it again, please."

This was the part that had enchanted me. The phrase had a kind of poise that seemed full of both certainty and uncertainty.

"Now," Madame said, "those notes in the left hand," she leaned over the keyboard and played the handful of notes like a growl, "you must imagine a sound that is no sound. You make them too distinct. That is not the character of this piece."

She had the student play the passage again and again. Occasionally Madame performed it again. "Forget you are playing the piano," she said. "This has nothing to do with the piano."

Her statement seemed outrageous to me, a heresy. I had believed her to have ultimate respect for the piano, just as I always told my English students that everything depended on language. Language was our instrument, I had said. Day after day, Madame had spoken of piano technique. But now she was saying forget the piano.

"With this," she went on, "this music has no body. This is music from beyond the grave. Not because it is *opus posthumous*—of course not. But because, finally, it is not human. You must go beyond that or you will never play it. Never."

She spoke with special patience, as though the cognitive meaning were important to her.

I was surprised when the next young Latin woman

played the same opus. I was more familiar with the piece now, and I could long for what I knew was coming and regret what was passing. If Joel had been with me, he would have had the same feeling.

In the middle of the performance, the stage and the entire auditorium were plunged in darkness. Apparently an electrical failure. It was total. I could see absolutely nothing; the only shape was the shape of darkness. But the performer continued as though nothing at all had happened. Not even at the moment when the lights went out was there the slightest discontinuity in the sound.

I heard Madame say quietly, "Nice." It was the only time she ever spoke while anyone was playing. The performer reached the end of the movement and went right on to the next. It seemed impossible that she could go on and on, but she did. She made no mistakes at all, though the blackness was so intense that I could not see the piano. In the middle of the second movement, the electricity came back on. I rather hated the brightness.

Madame said at the end, "Now you must tell me where you are from."

"Brazil."

"I knew it. The fire. Do you know German?"

The young woman shook her head in the negative, tossing her black hair, but Madame went on with her thought. "You play the middle section of the Andante sostenuto as though you know 'Der Lindenbaum' from *Die Winterreise*—'Komm her zumir, Geselle, hier findst Du rheine Ruh!' The linden tree is telling the unhappy lover, 'Come under my shadow and you will find your rest.'"

She went on to praise the performance and to make some slight suggestions. She never mentioned the blackout.

111

That night Terrel and I watched a number of grisly murders on the horror series, while Mother slept. During the commercials, I went out to the hall telephone and tried to get Joel, but he never answered. I seemed to leave myself, searching for him: I saw him in the back yard—out of earshot of the ringing phone—with a shovel, digging beside the patio; no, reaching up in the dark, with shears, snipping long branches off the elm.

Terrel and I began to test each other to see if it were all right to make fun of the film characters and the manner of their deaths.

Terrel casually put his arm around me. I let it stay; I pretended it wasn't there.

I was surprised that as I watched the screen, I was silently urging on the killer.

Four: The Lesson of Lust

Mother scribbled in my notebook: *What a beautiful face!*

I wrote back: *I don't think he's so special.*

He was a lanky young man, terribly American-looking after the international hodgepodge, with high cheekbones and a somewhat jutting jaw. Before he could get to the piano, Madame intercepted him and put her arm around him. She was grinning from ear to ear.

"And you also play the piano," she said. She turned to the audience, "I thought maybe he was a movie star."

The young man smiled as though he were used to such attentions. I glanced at Mother and she was beaming at the scene with an expression identical to Madame's. I didn't especially like his looks; that particular facial configuration had been one that I had loved on a certain man, a pianist even, who had made it clear that the passion was mostly on my side. Despite his having made me unhappy, those bones and angles belonged to his face, and I didn't like this man to have them.

Mother asked in my notebook: *Where is he from?*

While I was getting out the roster, Madame asked, "And where do you live?"

It turned out he was from Iowa.

"Not so far from here," Madame said. "You could come down once a month."

"I'd like to very much," he answered.

She squeezed him again, "Good. Very, very good. Now, what will you play?"

He spoke so quietly, just to her, that I couldn't hear his reply, but he performed the first movement of the Beethoven 109. I thought he played it quite well, and he did look rather romantic at the piano. His hair was dark, and he had a large nose, excellent for profile viewing.

As soon as he finished, Madame jumped up and hugged his shoulders. Then she put her hand on his head and said, "Wonderful, just wonderful." She was grinning all the time, as though she knew this was preposterous, but she intended to enjoy it just the same.

The young man seemed to realize that a stroke of uncommon fortune had come his way. I thought Joel played at least as well. Really Joel played more musically, though with less flash. Joel had a heart-shaped face and thick, rug-like hair. I loved his face, but I doubted it was one that would throw old ladies into ecstasy.

113

Mother wrote: *I bet she'd like to keep him!*

I wrote back: *She's already arranged for him to visit once a month.*

Mother insisted on the last word: *Fast work!*

That night I didn't go to the TV room or try to call Joel. I didn't want to find out that he wasn't home, or that he wouldn't come in from the back yard. I lay in bed and thought about my old beau with the high cheekbones, from the time after my divorce and before my second marriage. His touch was something my body could always remember. Once, back then, when I was going home alone from his place, and while I was walking across a footbridge, I had thought of him, and all the nerves in my body seemed to light up. It was as though an electric tree had sizzled inside my body. As I lay in the dorm bed in Oklahoma, I knew if I let my body remember, not just my mind, that again the tree would branch through me. I did let my body remember, and it was as though he had just touched me.

As I went to sleep I thought about how Madame's body probably remembered what it was to scrub floors. Probably some time when she stooped, perhaps to pick up a piece of music, her body remembered.

About three o'clock in the morning, I woke up because the room was stifling. Apparently there was another electrical failure and the air conditioning had gone off. I listened to Mother's breathing and hoped that she would sleep through the heat. We both lay still. After a while, I felt certain that she was awake and listening to me breathe, as I listened to her. Finally, she said, "Jackie, are you awake?"

I answered yes. The heat was incredible.

She said, "Get some wet towels. We'll take off our

114

gowns and wrap in the towels."

We did this, and the evaporation of the water cooled us. In the moonlight, with the towels bent to our shapes, we looked as though we were marble effigies. The wetness of the towel made me almost cold.

My thoughts turned to my teaching, and I remembered how once Mrs. Tibbs had said to me, "Jackie, the last year before I retire, would you teach *The Tempest*? I want to do that speech where Prospero breaks his staff and sinks his magic book." Just as spontaneously as I had laughed about her being Olivier, I had burst into tears.

After a while, Mother asked through the still air, "Did you talk to Joel lately?" and I answered, "Not lately."

When I woke up in the morning in the damp bed, I felt that we had survived an ordeal.

Five: The Lesson of Forgiveness

When the little Japanese boy approached the piano, I felt like writing to Mother in my notebook: *We don't have to watch this woman torture children; let's go.* But Mother didn't really know what happened with the other child. I could write: *I'm sick; let's go.* But Mother would be frightened. The auditorium air was warm and humid, threatening. A lavender band of flesh had appeared along the top of Mother's forehead just under the hairline.

Suddenly Mother took the notebook and wrote: *I hope she's nice to the little dear.*

I wrote back: *Isn't she always?*

Mother wrote: *I'll bet she could be nasty if she chose to.*

I let it go, but Mother insisted on another note: *I*

suppose he would certainly remind her of WWII prisoncamp experience?

Instead of sitting on the bench—the boy was so small—he leaned against it; his buttocks rested over its edge. His small tennis shoe reached out to locate the pedals, and his leg made a straight line from the bench to the floor. Paying no attention at all to Madame, he launched into the short, easy Grieg "Papillon."

From the opening chromatic run, resembling the flight of a butterfly, the performance took my breath. The child did not play like a child. He played the piece as though he were inventing it. I had heard a recording of Walter Gieseking playing a set of teaching pieces, and this was the way he had played "Papillon." No, the Japanese child played it better; every gesture had complete freshness and complete authority. Though it was a simple piece, the child's understanding of form and freedom in performance was absolute. It made me want to cry.

When he had finished, he stayed quietly leaning against the bench, his hands folded over his stomach; he did not look at Madame. She walked to him and touched his shoulders. Through her hands, she told him to stand up and to face us with her.

"Now," she said, "I can die."

She stood there quietly and bowed her head. Whether the child understood everything, understood nothing, I couldn't tell. She looked at us again.

"What you have heard—what you have had the privilege to hear—is a miracle. This little child has learned everything, and he already knows what we cannot teach him. None of us. Still, what my teacher gave to me, my wonderful teacher who gave me everything, everything, I

116

have given my student, and Kay has taught this child. Now the tradition has been passed on, and I can die."

Her bond was to the child, to a tradition in performance that, of course, I could never enter. And yet her bond was to me, too, because we had loved the same thing. Merely to forgive Joel seemed a slight thing.

Home

I thought that Joel would still be at work when we got home, but there was a strange car parked in the driveway. Neither Mother nor I mentioned it, but I went alone to the front door of my own home and rang the bell. Mother puttered around out at the car. I rather wished she were standing there with me, I remember.

While I waited for someone to appear, I stared at a muddy patch beside the door and realized that a new vine, a clematis, had been planted to grow on the mailbox—planted in an ugly and stupid way without any mulch. I looked at the large, rural-type mailbox where my tutored college students had left hundreds of their miserable essays—*without disturbing us, rain or shine,* I always said.

"Jackie!" Joel appeared. "Home safe!"

I was shocked to hear Mother, suddenly beside me, say, "Is everything all right?"

"Of course," Joel answered cheerfully.

We all hugged and walked into the house. While Mother was in the bathroom, I asked as lightly as I could, "Whose car?"

"Samantha's," he said. "I'll take it back tomorrow."

Numb, I managed finally to ask why it was here.

"She didn't want me to have to ride the bus to work." He didn't look at me when he spoke. He added, "Mr. Tibbs died while you were gone."

"Really?" I said, jarred. Still, I knew I was allowing him to distract me. "How is Mrs. Tibbs? Did you talk to her?"

He answered my questions, but I couldn't pay much attention. I wondered what piece of music I had been listening to in Oklahoma when Mrs. Tibbs saw that her husband was dead. I wondered if Joel had let Samantha lie on my side of the bed. I wondered about Mrs. Tibbs's state of mind—if I could help her in some way. I wondered if he had touched her the same ways he touched me—*yes*. And could he read her mind, the way he often did mine? *No*.

Joel took us into the back yard. He had bought a new Cape Hatteras hammock. I helped Mother lie down in the hammock, and Joel brought her the pillow embroidered with a treble clef.

"She looks perfect in the hammock, doesn't she?" he said to me.

I thought she looked like a fly in a web, but I could scarcely think of what to say. I felt that something long and difficult was beginning. Finally, I said, "I wish you could have heard what we heard."

"How did you like Madame," he asked, "in the end?"

"Better," I said. A group of white pansies held up their faces like smudged coins.

Joel looked at me quizically, expecting me to say more, trying to read my mood. I saw bitterly that I had become opaque to him.

"I'll get your mother some lemonade," he said.

I watched Mother take the glass from him. I had

been wrong in thinking that Mother disapproved of Joel in some obscure way. Not disapproval, but hope and affection were in her gaze as she looked at him, at us.

For her sake, I began to talk, said that in the end it didn't matter whether I liked Madame or not, suggested that Mother rest in the hammock while Joel and I fix a quick supper, that we eat outside on the blue slate patio.

While we munched the fried chicken, Mother happily told him about the performances we had heard, especially about the Schubert and the blackout and about the Grieg. She had never had such things to say to Robert.

The evening star was shining before we finished supper, and Joel helped Mother from the hammock into the house. "You've made everything so pretty," she said to him.

After he and I went to the living room, he turned on the lamps, sat down at the piano and played the Ravel *Pavane for a Dead Princess*. As always, the performance pleased me, comfortable as an old habit. He played as though he were playing just for me, as though, like the good lover he was, he knew just what I wanted. I couldn't stop myself from liking it, as I always had. Yet I thought of the waste of his talent, of his lack of commitment, with distaste.

Afterward, he rummaged in the music cabinet until he found the big Schubert sonata book. Then he turned off the lamps, except for a new little brass piano lamp he had bought while we were away. Suddenly I felt irrationally alarmed, but just before I could tell him not to, he began to read through the posthumous sonata.

As I sat patiently in the gloom, I decided it wasn't the mistakes, but, as Madame would have said, that the performance lacked fire. My eyes adjusted easily to the scant light, and I could see perfectly well. His allusion with this half-light to the pure blackness of the Brazilian performance seemed absurd.

When Mother and I had been alone in the yard for a moment, she had pulled me close and whispered, "Whose car is that in the driveway?" I had answered aloud, casually, "Just a friend's." Then I joked, "Don't worry, he didn't buy a new car," and she sank back on her pillow, relieved. I hoped that before she fell asleep in her room, she had not realized that she had allowed me to distract her.

How could Joel imagine that it was possible just to read through a piece like that? I was glad that Mother was already asleep and wouldn't hear his mistakes. Did he know that I would wait for her death, that he was safe till then?

I closed my eyes to imagine a complete blackness, a purer sound. And I felt again a connection with Madame and quietly said, "Nice."

I thought of Madame's energy while she scrubbed floors. How long did she wait for her liberation—two years? three? I sensed that she never lost confidence in her ability to wait, to emerge victorious.

The light from the piano lamp surrounded Joel in a soft cocoon. My gaze sailed the misty light, over the birds woven in the carpet, through a window.

Outside now, the scalloped leaves of a holly tree brush the window screen; beyond, the elm tree rises as a pattern in starlight.

I exist outside my living room, in music; noiseless and patient, my being dissolves, spins out fine as filament. Some place in Japan, on a winter afternoon, an aging man hears music from a piano, smiles, remembering briefly, how he liked to hear a prisoner playing, during the war.

120